THE BLACK PHD EXPERIENCE

Stories of Strength, Courage
and Wisdom in UK Academia

Edited by
William Ackah, Jacqueline Darkwa,
Wayne A. Mitchell, De-Shaine Murray
and Madina Wane

Foreword by
Jason Arday

First published in Great Britain in 2024 by

Policy Press, an imprint of
Bristol University Press
University of Bristol
1–9 Old Park Hill
Bristol
BS2 8BB
UK
t: +44 (0)117 374 6645
e: bup-info@bristol.ac.uk

Details of international sales and distribution partners are available at
policy.bristoluniversitypress.co.uk

© Bristol University Press 2024

British Library Cataloguing in Publication Data
A catalogue record for this book is available from the British Library

ISBN 978-1-4473-6997-4 hardcover
ISBN 978-1-4473-6998-1 paperback
ISBN 978-1-4473-6999-8 ePub
ISBN 978-1-4473-7000-0 ePdf

The right of William Ackah, Jacqueline Darkwa, Wayne A. Mitchell, De-Shaine Murray and Madina Wane to be identified as editors of this work has been asserted by them in accordance with the Copyright, Designs and Patents Act 1988.

All rights reserved: no part of this publication may be reproduced, stored in a retrieval system, or transmitted in any form or by any means, electronic, mechanical, photocopying, recording, or otherwise without the prior permission of Bristol University Press.

Every reasonable effort has been made to obtain permission to reproduce copyrighted material. If, however, anyone knows of an oversight, please contact the publisher.

The statements and opinions contained within this publication are solely those of the editors and contributors and not of the University of Bristol or Bristol University Press. The University of Bristol and Bristol University Press disclaim responsibility for any injury to persons or property resulting from any material published in this publication.

Bristol University Press and Policy Press work to counter discrimination on grounds of gender, race, disability, age and sexuality.

Cover design: Robin Hawes
Front cover image: Jacqueline Darkwa

Contents

Acronyms and glossary of terms	vii
Notes on contributors	ix
Acknowledgements	xiii
Foreword	xv
Jason Arday and Wayne A. Mitchell	
Introduction: Black PhD journeys in context	1
William Ackah	

PART I   **The 'weighted' waiting game: being Black and applying to do a PhD**   15
Wayne A. Mitchell

1. Underrepresented and undervalued: my reflections on school, university and the doctoral application process — 19
Sophie Martin

2. Climbing the rough side of the mountain: getting into a PhD programme — 23
Katty Wadda

3. What I wish I knew: deciding on when to pursue the PhD — 26
Esther Osarfo-Mensah

4. The long and winding road: tackling barriers and prejudice on the journey to PhD study — 31
Sigourney Bonner

5. Ignorance is not bliss: what every potential Black PhD science student needs to know — 35
Jason Amartey

6	Being one of the few among the many: my journey to the PhD starting point *Nina Higson-Sweeney*	40
7	Making the garments fit: transitions to a better place *Dwaynica Greaves*	44

Reflections on Part I and prompts for action 48
Wayne A. Mitchell

PART II	Being Black is not an optional luxury! Struggles for rights and recognition in the White academic space *Madina Wane*	49
8	Studying while Black: reflections on researching Blackness in White space *Alanah Mortlock*	53
9	Through, around or over the gate? Navigating academia from a Black Muslim woman's perspective *Amira Samatar*	57
10	Fighting the power: challenging institutional discrimination – a personal perspective *Hanna Akalu*	63
11	The missing ones	69

Reflections on Part II and prompts for action 70
Madina Wane

PART III	For us, by us: finding one another amid the storm *Jacqueline Darkwa*	71
12	That ain't it, so we'll create it: supporting Black students when and where our institutions fail *De-Shaine Murray*	75
13	Finding the Black immunologists in a pandemic *Madina Wane*	80

Contents

14	In the meantime: creating change through community *Paulette Williams*	85
15	Networks, networking and finding my place in the academic space *Deyl Djama*	90
16	#BlackInTheIvory: social media as a tool for racial healing *Louisa Brotherson*	93
17	Unravelling the tapestry of unspoken rules: living with being different in the academic space *Mary Agyapong*	98
18	Making space for Black voices and Black visions: the formation and work of the African Diaspora Postgraduate Network *William Ackah*	104

Reflections on Part III and prompts for action 109
Jacqueline Darkwa

PART IV	**Academic support: the right thing, in the right place, at the right time** *De-Shaine Murray*	111
19	Reaching beyond the horizon: being inspired to succeed against the odds *Simone Webb*	113
20	In and out of prison: my personal research journey of being a Black woman, researching Black women *Angela Charles*	118
21	Not in this alone: being supported to break down barriers to PhD success *Peggy Warren*	122
22	When seasons change: dealing with a change in my situation while studying for a PhD *Rees Johnson*	127

| 23 | Believing that the impossible is possible: my story of being supported to succeed
Clíona Kelly | 131 |

Reflections on Part IV and prompts for action 136
De-Shaine Murray

PART V	**Reflections at the completion of the PhD journey** *Madina Wane*	**137**
24	What it means to be the first: my journey from Windrush to PhD *Julia Morris*	141
25	Why the 'P' in PhD stands for (Black) Power *April-Louise Pennant*	146
26	(Un)making the imposter syndrome *Barbara Adewumi*	152
27	I came all this way for this?! An international student's experience of UK higher education *Anon*	157

Reflections on Part V and prompts for action 162
Madina Wane

Conclusion and recommendations 163
De-Shaine Murray

Our ancestors' wildest dreams ... (fictionalisation) 176
Jacqueline Darkwa

Afterword: For our community 179
De-Shaine Murray

Index 180

Acronyms and glossary of terms

A-level	Advanced level
ADPN	African Diaspora Postgraduate Network
BA	Bachelor of Arts
BAME	Black, Asian and minority/minoritised ethnic
Black	African-descendant individuals of Caribbean/West Indian, African and/or mixed heritage
BSc	Bachelor of Science
BTEC	Business and Technology Education Council
CDT	Centre for doctoral training
CRT	Critical Race Theory
DPhil	The award of a PhD specifically from University of Oxford
DTP	Doctoral training programme
GCSE	General Certificate of Secondary Education
HEI	Higher education institution
MA	Master of Arts
MPhil	Master of Philosophy
MRes	Master of Research
MSc	Master of Science
MSci	Master in Science
NHS	National Health Service
O-Level	Ordinary level
Oxbridge	Collective term for University of Oxford and University of Cambridge
PGR	Postgraduate researcher
PhD	Doctorate of Philosophy
PI	Principal investigator
SFE	Student Finance England
STEM	Science, Technology, Engineering and Mathematics

UCAS	Universities and Colleges Admissions Service – the national UK application service for undergraduate and taught postgraduate degrees
UKRI	United Kingdom Research and Innovation

Notes on contributors

William Ackah is Senior Lecturer in Black and Community Geographies at Birkbeck, University of London. He gained his PhD in Government at the University of Manchester in 2006. He is the current chair of the Transatlantic Roundtable on Religion and Race and a co-convenor of the African Diaspora Postgraduate Network. He is a Fulbright research scholar and has published widely in the areas of African Diaspora politics, religion and culture. He is currently completing a monograph *Black space matters: resisting the erasures of Black cultures and communities*, to be published by Bloomsbury.

Barbara Adewumi is Senior Research Fellow, University of Kent. Research interests include sociology, race, equality and progression in higher education.

Mary Agyapong is Doctoral Researcher at King's College London and co-founder of the West African Research Collective. Research interests include autism, ADHD, neurodevelopment.

Hanna Akalu is Doctoral Researcher at Glasgow Caledonian University. Research interests include social justice, inequalities, intersectionality, islamophobia, community-led participatory research.

Jason Amartey is Doctoral Researcher at University of Nottingham. Research interests include cardiovascular diseases.

Sigourney Bonner (née Bell) is Doctoral Researcher at University of Cambridge, Cancer Research UK and CEO of Black in Cancer. Research interests include paediatric brain tumours.

Louisa Brotherson is Doctoral Researcher at University of Liverpool. Research interests include Seismology and Rock Deformation.

Angela Charles is Lecturer at Northampton University. Research interests include race, gender and the criminal justice system.

Jacqueline Darkwa is an education advocate and visual storyteller. She graduated from Imperial College London, 2019, in MSc Science Communication. Her research interests cover the intersection of race, gender and identity with science, as well as social justice. She is a documentary photographer and filmmaker of Ghanaian heritage.

Deyl Djama is Doctoral Researcher at the Imperial College London. Research interests include neuroscience.

Dwaynica Greaves is Doctoral Researcher at University College London. Research interests include theatre-neuroscience and social cognition.

Nina Higson-Sweeney is Lecturer at the University of Bath. Research interests include child and adolescent mental health, qualitative methods, open science, equality and diversity, and lived experience perspectives.

Rees Johnson is Lecturer at the University of Essex. Research interests include end of life and assisted dying.

Clíona Kelly is Postdoctoral Fellow at Yale University. Research interests include social interaction, the maternal brain, virtual reality and electroencephalography.

Sophie Martin is Doctoral Researcher at University College London. Research interests include artificial intelligence for medical imaging.

Wayne A. Mitchell is Joint Associate Provost for Equality, Diversity and Inclusion and Principal Teaching Fellow and Senior Tutor at Imperial College London. Graduating from the

Notes on contributors

University of Birmingham with a degree in Biomedical Science, he completed a PhD at University College London in Molecular Genetics, before undertaking postdoctoral positions in Cancer Biology and Immunology. He has always been interested in understanding what makes students learn and has taught at all levels of the British education system. He completed a Master's in Education at Imperial College focusing on the experiences of Black British students at elite universities and how their 'minority status' impacts on their sense of belonging and identity.

Julia Morris is a healthcare research and data analyst at Clarivate. Research interests include oncology.

Alanah Mortlock is Doctoral Researcher at the London of School Economics. Research interests: Black feminist theory, racial ambivalence, critiques of identity.

De-Shaine Murray is Wu Tsai Institute Postdoctoral Fellow at Yale University. He gained his PhD in Bioengineering from Imperial College London in 2022, creating devices to monitor the injured brain. While obtaining this degree he founded and co-founded various groups, including the African-Caribbean Research Collective, West African Research Collective, Black In Neuro, Imperial College London Black Doctoral Network to support students locally, regionally and globally.

Esther Osarfo-Mensah is Doctoral Researcher at University College London. Research interests include Biosensors.

April-Louise Pennant is Leverhulme Trust Early Career Fellow at Cardiff University. Research interests include sociology, social justice, education, history, heritage and memory.

Amira Samatar is Doctoral Researcher at Sheffield Hallam University. Research interests include educational journeys and trajectories of racially minoritised groups.

Katty Wadda is Doctoral Researcher at the University of Cambridge. Research interests include infectious diseases.

Madina Wane is a medical research professional and community organiser. She gained her PhD in Immunology from Imperial College London in 2021 and has since worked in the biotechnology and medical research charity sectors. Madina's research interests include immunology and the intersection of social justice and science. She co-founded a non-profit organisation, Black In Immuno, to address the inequities facing Black scientists within the field of immunology and has engaged in other initiatives on equity, policy, and racism in science.

Peggy Warren is a director at Phencheater Charles Ltd. Research interests include women's studies/performative methodologies.

Simone Webb is Research Associate at Newcastle University. Research interests include developmental biology, bioinformatics, immunology and neurobiology.

Paulette Williams is founder and CEO of Leading Routes. Research interests include education.

One of the contributors is anonymous by request.

Acknowledgements

We would like to acknowledge the many Black PhD students, past and present, who have contributed to this work, those inside the book and those whose words and activities influenced our thinking. A special thank you to Paulette Williams and Leading Routes, whose pioneering efforts on behalf of Black postgraduates has been truly inspirational, Monique Charles and Antoinette Kwegan for establishing the Black Doctoral Network UK branch, another pioneering effort in support of Black PhD students, and Nkasi Stoll, who provided valuable resources to support the wellbeing of contributors. We would like to acknowledge and thank the many Black academics who, through their work and activism, have paved the way for so many students to take the journey to doctoral studies. There are far too many to mention individually, but we would particularly like to recognise the foundational work of Professor Hakim Adi and the young historians project for their efforts in championing the cause of Black postgraduate students in History. We would also like to recognise the contribution of independent Black scholars and Black publishers who paved the way for us in community spaces and supplementary schools and published work such as Bernard Coard's influential *How the West Indian child is made educationally sub-normal in the British school system*. We extend a big thank you to Policy Press, in particular Paul Stevens and Isobel Green, for believing in us and this project.

William Ackah would like to acknowledge the work of Professor Robert Beckford and Dr Gabrielle Beckles-Raymond, whose founding and support of the African Diaspora Postgraduate Network has empowered countless students over the years and whose ideas have influenced thinking in the book. He would also like to thank Leon Tikly and Marge Malcolm for their comments and suggestions on the text. Also, the Ackah and Banjo families for their support.

Finally, he would also like to thank his dear wife Helena for her comments and unwavering support throughout the project.

De-Shaine Murray would like to thank his family for their unwavering support. He would like to acknowledge the communities that are guiding the next set of Black academics, including the African Caribbean Research Collective, West African Research Collective, Black In Neuro and Imperial College London Black Doctoral Network, who have been an integral part of his journey and inspiration. He would also especially like to thank his wife Clíona for being an anchor and constant source of support.

Wayne A. Mitchell would like to thank his family for their continual support, encouragement, and for allowing him the time and space to engage in the development and delivery of this project. To the many guests who have shared their lived experiences as part of Imperial As One's Belonging interview series and how their contributions inspire some others to believe they can achieve. For BlackAdemic for their positive vibes and being the watcher who provide warnings, advice and guidance for this and future generations. Finally, he would like to thank his BFF ZGTM, for her love, support and always believing that together we are more than!

Jacqueline Darkwa would like to thank all scholars who have dedicated their time to exploring the realities of the Black experience in academia; their work may have gone under the radar, but never undervalued. She would also like to thank friends and family who have supported her on this journey, in particular her grandparents, who have been her guiding force. Finally, she would like to thank the Black community for continuing to be her inspiration in times of great strife and suffering, teaching her how to find joy.

Madina Wane would like to thank the collaborators and friends who have been a consistent source of support, provide a space to share frustrations, and encourage her to dream of worlds beyond oppressions. She is particularly grateful for the team at Black In Immuno, the West African Research Collective, Nuzhat, Nirmz and Supreet. She also thanks her parents who instilled in her a deep appreciation of learning and her ancestors whose legacies continue to teach her new lessons every day. So dole kebbi yo dole kebbo. Finally, she thanks those who provided valuable feedback on this project, including Mamadou, Faith, Shomari and Yolanda.

Foreword

Jason Arday and Wayne A. Mitchell

We are often told that there is a pipeline and that it is leaking, a pipeline that needs to be fixed, made more inclusive with initiatives that support individuals from diverse communities. Could it be that the pipeline is perfectly fine, however those regulating the release valves are selectively choosing what (who) can and cannot pass through their pipes? The *Black PhD Experience: Stories of Strength, Courage and Wisdom in UK Academia* provides 27 illuminating insights into the PhD journeys of Black students. The narratives ask the questions: Why are talented Black students having to wait longer to be accepted into PhD programmes? Where are the institutional support systems, mentor programmes, supervisors, champions and role models to nurture and provide the guidance that our Black students need to thrive? Why is academia so hostile to Black success? Is it time for the Black community to unite to gain greater knowledge and understanding of these academic systems to better support our young people or consider developing our own support networks?

In the five years since the release of the seminal report, *The broken pipeline*, by Black-led organisation Leading Routes, there has been a seismic shift in efforts challenging the institutional and systemic racisms, not only in academia but beyond. The increasing number of interventions being promoted and importantly funded by UK funding bodies, universities and influential individuals in the Black community can assist in mobilising the trajectory of early career Black scholars. These efforts to encourage greater success and pathways into academia have seen the development of programmes enabling more access to different types of knowledge, and better tools to navigate the thorny landscape of the academy and its marginalising and exclusionary ways. What these 27 stories provide is an opportunity to really understand the lived experience that these Black PhD students have encountered, endured, and overcome on their journeys.

Unfortunately, as all societies are governed by the policies of their time, hostile forces opposed to anti-racism continue to *shout* in an attempt to silence and undermine these efforts. Furthermore, we need to recognise that the instruments of racism act on a swivel; they can realign, adapt and remodel at any given time. So we need to develop stable, flexible systems to combat these changes. The more they *shout*, the *stronger* our communities need to grow. More unity in the community is required and it is imperative that we act with one voice. We need to be active pipeline inspectors, continuously evaluating university policies and procedures, criteria, requesting data in terms of the numbers of Black students who are not only getting onto PhDs but being provided with viable and equitable academic careers. We need to hold institutions accountable. Beyond the PhD we need to see more opportunities for better engagement and representation throughout every stage of the academic pipeline, more Black postdocs, more Black lecturers, more Black senior lecturers, more Black readers, more Black professors, and more Black senior leaders. We need more!

The impact of systemic institutionalised racism is real and permeates the very fabrics of our edifices of education. We are sick and tired of hearing about your intentions. So, as this text boldly argues, no more performative statements – we need to see intentional concrete actions that recognise the needs of Black and other underrepresented groups. For many Black scholars, these accounts will be reminiscent of their own experiences, and it is time that the leaders of universities and funding bodies act with intentionality to reflect the courage, strength and wisdom demonstrated by the Black PhD students in this book.

Finally, it is hugely important that we recognise that Black excellence has transpired in spite of what still remains a largely exclusionary and racist system. For anyone wanting to truly understand the experience of the Black PhD student, this book is a 'must-read'. While advances are being made, this is an opportunity for us to reflect and imagine the success through the experiences of these 27 amazing scholars. Let us celebrate their achievements.

Introduction: Black PhD journeys in context

William Ackah

What is it like to be a Black postgraduate student in the United Kingdom (UK)? A simple question for an academic text to answer, you may think. What may seem straightforward on the surface, however, is anything but. The Black postgraduate student experience is a complex mixture of hope, audacity, expectation, disappointment, rage, sacrifice and dreams fulfilled and unfulfilled. It is also part of the wider Black community experience in Britain, one that has been forged over the centuries through blood, sweat and tears (Olusoga, 2016). As bell hooks outlines:

> I am grateful to the many women and men who dare to create theory from the location of pain and struggle, who courageously expose wounds to give us their experience to teach and guide, as a means to chart new theoretical journeys. Their work is liberatory. (hooks, 1994, p. 74)

The Black PhD Experience: Stories of Strength, Courage and Wisdom in UK Academia is our collective endeavour to share the complex and multi-layered experiences of Black students in the UK as they go through the process of obtaining the highest academic qualification, the Doctorate of Philosophy (PhD). It is a book, but it is more than merely a text: it is an experience. As the pages move you will be drawn into an immersive, emotional kaleidoscope of thoughts, feelings and tangible expressions of Black humanity. We want you, as readers, to walk with us, to see the higher education system through our eyes and to understand where we have come from to reach this place. Ours is not a traditional 'how to do x and y' textbook; there are excellent works outlining the what, where and how of tackling institutionalised racism in higher education (Verma, 2022) and we will refer to them at points on the journey. There are, however, more fundamental issues at stake for us than just showing people how to treat us equitably in universities and colleges. The heinous murder of George Floyd in May 2020 in the United States of America (US) was a powerful wake-up call for Black people all over the world and had particular resonances for Black students and scholars in the UK. The who of who we are and the where of where we come from is inextricably linked to how we get mis/treated in British society and, in particular, the higher education system. The racism at the heart of this system puts our lives on the line. We may not get choked to death in broad daylight on the street, but constant undermining and everyday dealing with racist microaggressions does inevitably drain the air from your body.

In this system we are designated as (non)humans, and are often reduced to a statistical anomaly that is deemed fixable by a widening participation programme, a positive action initiative, mentoring scheme or race equality training package. How much research needs to be produced, reports written, symposia held before higher education institutions recognise that Black students are not the problem, the system is! When will they wake up and implement the necessary changes that genuinely respect and appreciate Black student experiences in all their diversities and specificities.

This book was challenging to produce and it will be challenging to read in places because in it we are honest and vulnerable. Each editor and contributor knows what it is like to be visible yet invisible within the British higher education system. We have seen our images on the glossy advertising brochure selling us an illusory dream of inclusivity. We have experienced slights, rejections, downgrades, neglect and harassment and, when we have chosen to speak up, we have been told it is down to our lack of ability that we experience what we experience! Negativity is not the whole story. We have also experienced the highs of gaining acceptance into prestigious institutions, the thrills of having papers accepted for publication and the sheer joy and delight of graduating in front of friends and family in cap and gown, PhD in hand. Our lived experiences are complex, reflective of a complicated relationship with higher education institutions. We are not reducible to a single story (Adiche, 2009) but our combined narratives do illuminate the fact that higher education in the UK has a collective institutionalised racism problem that needs eradicating urgently (Arday and Mirza, 2018).

As editors we have been struck by the fact that the dominant narrative of Black people in Britain that emanates from the political classes and the media is that of either being useful to society or a problem. Our issues in higher education are part and parcel of this deeper historical dichotomy that runs through British society whereby we are either good contributors to Britain or a problematic drain (Hirsch, 2018). As the descendants of enslaved and colonised people our positionality in Britain has primarily been based on our worth or value rather than our intrinsic humanity (Ramdin, 1987; Beckles, 2013). Our bodies as free labour were most useful in the development of plantation economics through the fifteenth to nineteenth centuries, making Britain rich. But our minds were a problem, so access to reading and writing was forbidden or severely curtailed. We were assessed, studied and labelled as inferior beings by intellectuals working in universities (Ackah, 2021)!

In the colonial era of the nineteenth and early twentieth centuries, when the British empire was at its height, our lands and resources were extracted of their value to make the 'Great' in Great Britain (Andrews, 2021). Our productive capacity was very useful. We, as people from the colonies, however, were problems to be controlled, with higher education providing the tools to manage and govern 'problematic natives'. Elite institutions such as the School of Oriental and African Studies and Imperial College London gained their names and esteem on the backs of the colonisation of Black minds and bodies.

When Britain won the Second World War, but lost its empire in the aftermath, it continued in its treatment of its Black populations as either useful and/or problematic, as it used its former colonial subjects to rebuild its shattered economy. So, we were useful to clean the hospitals, conduct the buses, toil in the factories and do the labour that others were not willing to do. As our parents and grandparents began to settle and started to want more for themselves they/we became a problem. We were difficult to educate, problematic to house, criminal minded, too numerous, too disruptive, we were a problem (Gilroy, 1987).

This dichotomy has persisted into the twenty-first century. In education, Black school students are the most likely to be excluded and sent to pupil referral units (Graham, 2016). Black people are far more likely to be imprisoned than their White counterparts (Lammy, 2017). Black people are more likely to be misdiagnosed in hospital and die prematurely than the majority White population. In almost every socio-economic indicator that speaks to how a nation looks after its citizens, from health to housing, education to employment, Black people experience poor treatment, inadequate services and have the worst outcomes (Byrne et al., 2020). Yet, in the midst of this inequitable treatment, our communities are still working for the benefit of the country, fighting in wars, looking after the sick, populating the universities, paying our taxes and making sacrificial contributions over and above the call of duty.

If this book were being written in 1904, this inequitable state of affairs would be unjust. If we were describing said scenarios and conditions in 1954 it would be deeply problematic. The fact that this is being written in 2024 is a stinging indictment that Britain has failed to deal with one of its most pressing issues. The country has a drug problem – it has an ongoing addiction to the exploitation of its Black population and that is downright inhumane. The country and its institutions still struggle to see us as human equals and is continually caught in this vicious cycle of regarding us as either good, useful immigrants or as problems (Shukla, 2016). It does not want to recognise that, as a society, it is the one that has a deep-seated racism problem. COVID-19 provided a very clear example of this. Black, Asian and other minoritised ethnic groups were overrepresented in the healthcare professions, taking care of the sick and the vulnerable of the nation. This was us at our useful best. However, at the same time, Black, Asian and minoritised bodies were getting sick and dying at higher rates than their White counterparts, and we were a problem. The perception was that what we ate, where and how we lived meant that we were more susceptible to the virus and would spread it. The structural factors impacting Black health outcomes, including the racism of the National Health Service, was conveniently forgotten. When academic research councils gave out millions of pounds in grants on COVID-19 disparities, Black researchers were nowhere to be seen (Adelaine, 2020). We were the non-humans, denied agency even when our community was dying! We make no apologies for including this here; we are our community, and as they experience dehumanisation on account of being Black so do we. bell hooks again is very insightful for us on this: 'It is crucial and necessary for insurgent black intellectuals to have an ethics of struggle that informs our relationship to those black people who have not had access to ways of knowing shared in locations of privilege' (hooks, 1994, p. 54).

The discourses that position Global Black Majority people as minoritised, immigrants, ethnic minorities, lends itself to a social and policy environment that deems us as problems to be solved or issues to be dealt with. In higher education specifically this comes out as developing special measures to either widen access for or lift up the attainment levels of Black students so that we can be like the 'rest' of society. This absolves the nation and the system that underpins it of its role in creating such an inequitable and unjust set of practices in the first place. As editors we want to fundamentally challenge and dismantle the idea that we as Black students and academics are somehow 'less than', and that 'our' issues can be fixed with a little helping hand from a benign higher education system.

To all who are reading this text, let us make this abundantly clear: Black people are not a problem. As the voices in this collection will testify, we are intelligent, sophisticated, nuanced and dedicated, just like every other minority or majority ethnic community in this country. We should not have to spell this out and continually repeat it on these pages, but the sad truth is that, unless we shout, challenge and continually raise these points, we will continue to be patronised and then ignored.

We set out this contextual framing so that it is clear that it is the UK and its institutions that are the problem. They have been instrumental in treating Black people as commodities to be used and abused. Some institutionalised spaces are less pronounced in their extractive methods than others, but overall the evidence is overwhelming, Britain treats its Black population as less than. This is the analytical framing and context out of which our contributor voices speak. This is the Britain whose waters Black student bodies have to navigate. One of the most challenging and unpredictable aspects of these spaces is that of higher education to which we now turn our attention to specifically.

Higher education: a special case?

The higher education space positions itself as somehow different from the rest of British institutional life. It believes that its space is liberal and tolerant, where anyone can succeed based on merit. It promotes the ideas of core values, integrity, fairness, justice and making decisions based on evidence and reason. In such a space it is unlikely, according to the internal wisdom, that racism would be a serious problem, if it existed at all. Higher education exists somewhat in a bubble; it will conduct research and offer wisdom on events outside of itself but very rarely will it critically interrogate its own actions, particularly as it applies to issues of race and the experience of Black students (Arday, 2018). The multiple first-hand accounts in this work will burst this internal bubble.

The story of the liberal meritocratic university has been exposed as a fallacy, especially in relation to Black communities. Elite universities discriminate against some communities when it comes to gaining places at their institutions (Boliver, 2016). Institutions from across the teaching and research spectrum practise discrimination in awarding certain ethnic categories higher degree classifications than others (Arday et al., 2022). Black graduates are less likely to find employment than their White counterparts (Petrie, 2021). Black students are far less likely to be provided with a funded opportunity to undertake postgraduate studies than their White counterparts (Williams et al., 2019). Discriminatory practices exist at every level of academia. At the top of the pyramid the results are plain to see; the number of Black individuals who head institutions as vice-chancellors is in single figures and the number of Black professors in the UK is less than 200 in an eligible cohort of over 20,000.

Introduction

The university, rather than being a beacon of equality and integrity, reveals itself to be a bastion of coloniality and privilege (Bhopal & Myers, 2023). In recent times, this privilege and the legacies of enslavement and colonialism enshrined in academic institutions has begun to be challenged. Black students, in increasing numbers, are entering the space of the university and forcing reconsiderations of what the university is for. What should be studied? Who should be venerated and revered? And how should the benefits and prestige accrued on the backs of Black bodies and minds be adequately accounted for? (Ackah, 2021). The horrific murder of George Floyd and the power of the Black Lives Matter Movement to bring the centrality of Black experiences into the public square has created an impetus to rethink the university (Harney & Moten, 2013; Jansen, 2019). Global Black Majority students are leading the way, seeking to change an unjust system while they navigate their way through it. Rhodes Must Fall, Fees Must Fall, Why Is My Curriculum White, Why Isn't My Professor Black were some of the contemporary iterations of attempts to change the nature of higher education by Global Black Majorities (Bhambra et al., 2018; Rhodes Must Fall, 2018).

Black in the White educational space

If the university is so bad and not conducive for Black students to learn in an anti-racist and just environment, why persist? For all its problems, the university is still regarded as a space of opportunity and a place to explore ideas and develop new knowledge. Universities are also spaces of power and influence and Black people, so long shut out of such spaces, feel that, when given the opportunity, they should take advantage of it. At the height of British colonialism young Black men and women came from the colonies to study in universities in the UK, the US and mainland Europe. In the midst of prejudice and racism, they found space to understand their colonial oppressors and to develop ideas and ways of thinking and knowing that would ultimately lead to independence for nations in Africa, the Caribbean and Asia (Adi, 1998; Gopal, 2019). Others were not so revolutionarily inclined; but they studied and became doctors, lawyers, media workers and more, contributing to the life of the nation and being the precursors of those who would embed more forcefully diversity into the British landscape after the Second World War.

The stories of Black students in British universities before the Second World War and the early days of post-war migration does need more telling on its own terms; but we raise it here to provide background and context for understanding the contemporary experiences of Black postgraduate students in Britain. The early student pioneers occupied a liminal space in British society, between the worlds of privileged elite education and that of being a marginalised minority part of Britain's fledging Black and minority ethnic community. The combination of access to knowledge and privilege, while seeing and experiencing the horrendous racism that stemmed from being a descendant of the colonised and enslaved in the land of the coloniser, elicited a complex set of responses in those who were exposed to these spaces – a mixture of admiration and revulsion. In the colonial space there was a desire to succeed, to demonstrate that the racist portrayals of your countries and peoples were inaccurate. There was also a burden of representation – a need to show one's community what success looked like and that the qualifications attained would lead to something positive, both for the individual and the community (Ackah, 1999, pp. 1–13).

The terrain may have altered, but the legacies of enslavement and colonialism still pervade the institutional set-ups of higher education systems in Britain. Black students still face dilemmas. How much should they give of themselves to institutions steeped in racism? What do they owe their communities? And how should they repay them?

A key component of the colonial education system and its attempted impact on the Black intellectual was to try and separate the individual from their community. This took the form of belittling the culture and wisdom of the community and by creating strict demarcations concerning what constituted academic knowledge and ways of knowing what was outside that domain. The religions, histories and cultures of Black communities had to be disregarded or relegated to a footnote if one was to enter academia. This was at the root of the intellectual agenda of the colonial project as directed at educated Black elites (WA Thiong'o,

1986). Its continued legacy has been felt in education systems across Africa and the diaspora (Tikly, 2020).

An important lesson that has shaped our thinking is that, as Black students and academics, we must maintain links between ourselves and our communities. A key component of Black educational endeavour must be a conscious decision to expand the spaces of Black solidarity and support for education. We must not be cut off from our communities in some spurious pursuit of academic excellence. We recognise the dilemmas faced by intellectuals, but we are nothing without our communities. Our past, present and future rest on our relationship to communities of praxis. As they go, so we go.

Higher education needs to be opened up, access must be reframed, moving from focusing on the Black individual to appreciating and valuing Black communities and placing them at the heart of knowledge production. Universities that have caused so much damage to our communities through their racist theorising and dehumanising practices must repair the damage they have caused and restore value and esteem to our communities.

The postgraduate student also has to be reimagined to account for the lifelong and interdisciplinary learning that permeates the Black experience. As this work will attest, we are striving and struggling to get through the system as it is currently constructed. But we want to do more than survive; we want to flourish and thrive. To do that, we need more space to enable us to think, conjure and transform an individualised, hierarchical, mystical master, tutor model of postgraduate learning to a more communal, transparent, inclusive model that nurtures and respects Black humanity in all its forms. This is our fundamental right as Black British students navigating the educational system and, as the book will outline, a better system for Black people will be a system better for everyone.

Methodology

The Black PhD Student Experience in the UK was born out of discussions between past and present Black students undertaking doctoral studies. The editors, in our various capacities, had become deeply frustrated by the policy initiatives that were being introduced to promote diversity and to support students from Black, Asian and minority ethnic backgrounds. We put out a call through our Black support networks and wider Black community forums to invite past and present students to talk and write about their experiences. In 2020–21 we held a series of online focus groups, where our participants shared their ideas and experiences; and from these reasoning sessions we developed a framework and asked people to share their thoughts for publication. We initially had 30 concrete expressions of interest from participants who wanted to write but, due to various factors, this was brought down to 24. We then invited three additional contributors who organised Black support networks to contribute to the text. At a late stage, we lost a valuable contribution which also starkly highlighted for us the challenges known and unknown faced by Black doctoral students, which we hope will be addressed as a result of this work. This left us with the 26 contributions that you will read. We liaised with our participants throughout the process of production, showing them the themes as they emerged from their submissions and seeking their views on recommendations for the sector. So, what you see before you is a collective endeavour and not solely the work of the editors. The students past and present are all Black – African descendants of Caribbean/West Indian, African and/or mixed heritage – and they come from a range of subject areas and disciplines so that the fullest range of Black experiences that we could gather is present in the text. There is one international student experience in the text; all the rest are resident Black British experiences. The students come from a range of backgrounds in regards to class, gender, ability/disability and sexuality and, as you read their accounts, the intersectional dimensions of their lived experience and the barriers that they have encountered will be evident (Crenshaw et al., 2024). Black student lives are textured and nuanced, but race is still central; as Walter Rodney famously outlined: 'Black Power is a doctrine about black people, for black people, preached by black people. I'm putting it to my black brothers and sisters that the colour of our skins is the most fundamental thing about us' (Rodney, 1975, p. 16).

A limitation of this work is that it does not contain the experiences of students who were put off from applying for a

PhD or of those who did not complete. We hope that this will be addressed in a future project. The experiences of the contributors are all first-hand accounts; we did not dictate to contributors what they should write; our framing, analysis recommendations and conclusions come from reading their accounts and analysing them alongside data and other reports and research on the Black student experience in the UK.

Layout and themes

Our book follows the lifecycle of the Black postgraduate student experience from pre-application through to graduation and beyond. The introduction sets out the rationale and framing of the overall volume with its challenge to immerse oneself in the humanity of the Black student experience and to view the student experience within the context of the Black community experience past, present and future. Part I, 'The "weighted" waiting game', details the varied experiences of students as they contemplated and eventually took the plunge to apply to enter the Ivory Tower of higher education. Part II, 'Being Black is not an optional luxury!', follows students as they experience studying for a PhD and wrestle with issues of supervision, imposter syndrome, institutionalised racism and struggles of health and wellbeing. Part III, 'For us, by us – finding one another amid the storm', focuses on the role of Black support networks in the life journeys of students. Here the presence of the wider Black community is highlighted as being of crucial importance in bolstering the individual in pursuit of their qualification. Part IV, 'Academic support', focuses on the role of institutional and individual support in the life of the PhD student. Contributors testify to the importance of supportive supervisors and of institutions that believe in the intrinsic worth of their students. In Part V, 'Reflections at the completion of the PhD journey', PhD graduates reflect on their journeys, the highs and lows of their traversals through the system and the experience of life beyond graduation. Each section is prefaced by a contextualised introduction that enables the reader to connect the testimonies of the individual contributors to a broader community framework. The text ends with recommendations, conclusions and imaginings. What does a Black PhD student experience look and feel like within an environment that respects the student's humanity and the community from which they emanate? What does it mean to embrace the Black community and repair the damage caused by the legacies of enslavement, colonialism and the contemporary manifestations of institutionalised racism?

We want to envisage a future free from racism and our hope is that, as you read this text and immerse yourself in the Black PhD student experience, you will work toward that future with us.

References

Ackah, W. (1999). *Pan-Africanism: exploring the contradictions: politics, identity and development in Africa and the African diaspora.* Aldershot: Ashgate.

Ackah, W. (2021). 'From ethnic minorities to Black majorities: the challenges and dilemmas of attempting to decolonize the British education system', *The Peabody Journal of Education,* 96(2), 192–205.

Adelaine, A. et al. (2020). 'Knowledge is power: an open letter to UKRI Research Professional News'. https://www.researchprofessionalnews.com/rr-news-uk-views-of-the-uk-2020-8-knowledge-is-power-an-open-letter-to-ukri/ (accessed 22 November 2023).

Adi, H. (1998). *West Africans in Britain 1900–1960: nationalism, pan-Africanism and communism.* London: Lawrence & Wishart.

Adiche, C.N. (2009). 'The danger of a single story', TED TALK, YouTube. https://www.youtube.com/watch?v=D9Ihs241zeg (accessed 25 September 2023).

Andrews, K. (2021). *The new age of empire: how racism and colonialism still rule the world.* London: Penguin Books.

Arday, J. (2018). 'Understanding racism within the academy: the persistence of racism within higher education'. In A. Johnson, R. Joseph-Salisbury and B. Kamunge (eds), *The Fire Now: Anti-Racist Scholarship in Times of Explicit Racial Violence.* London: Zed, pp. 26–37.

Arday, J., Branchu, C. and Boliver, V. (2022). 'What Do we know about Black and minority ethnic (BAME) participation in higher education', *Social Policy and Society,* 21(1), 12–25.

Arday, J. and Mirza, H.S. (eds) (2018). *Dismantling race in higher education.* London: Palgrave Macmillan.

Beckles, H. (2013). 'Not human: Britain's Black property'. In *Britain's Black debt: reparations for Caribbean slavery and native genocide.* Kingston: University of the West Indies, pp. 56–67.

Bhambra, G.K., Gebriel, D. and Nisancioglu, K. (eds) (2018). *Decolonising the university.* London: Pluto.

Bhopal, K. and Myers, M. (2023). *Elite universities and the making of privilege.* Oxford: Routledge.

Boliver, V. (2016). 'Exploring ethnic inequalities in admission to Russell Group universities', *Sociology,* 50(2), 247–66.

Byrne, B., Alexander, C., Khan, O., Nazroo, J. and Shankley, W. (2020). *Ethnicity, race and inequality in the UK.* Bristol: Policy.

Crenshaw, K., Andrews, K. and Wilson, A. (eds) (2024). *Blackness at the intersection.* London: Bloomsbury.

Gilroy, P. (1987). *There ain't no Black in the Union Jack: the cultural politics of race and nation.* London: Unwin Hyman.

Gopal, P. (2019). *Insurgent empire: anti-colonial resistance and British dissent.* London: Verso.

Graham, K. (2016). 'The British school to prison pipeline'. In K. Andrews and L.A. Palmer, *Blackness in Britain.* Oxford: Routledge.

Harney, S. and Moten, F. (2013). *The undercommons: fugitive planning and Black study.* London: Minor Compositions.

Hirsch, A. (2018). *BRIT (ISH) On race, identity and belonging.* London: Jonathan Cape.

hooks, b. (1994). *Teaching to transgress: education as the practice of freedom.* New York: Routledge.

Jansen, J. (ed.) (2019). *Decolonisation in universities: the politics of knowledge.* Johannesburg: Wits University.

Lammy, D. (2017). *The Lammy Review: an independent review into the treatment of, and outcomes for, Black, Asian and Minority Ethnic individuals in the Criminal Justice System.* https://assets.publishing.service.gov.uk/media/5a82009040f0b62305b91f49/lammy-review-final-report.pdf.

Olusoga, D. (2016). *Black and British: a forgotten history.* London: Macmillan.

Petrie, K. (2021). *Graduate outcomes in London.* London: Social Market Foundation.

Ramdin, R. (1987). *The making of the Black working class in Britain.* Aldershot: Wildwood House.

Rhodes Must Fall, Oxford (2018). *Rhodes Must Fall: the struggle to decolonise the racist heart of empire.* London: Zed.

Rodney, W. (1975). *The groundings with my brothers,* 2nd edn. London: Bogle-L'ouverture.

Shukla, N. (ed.) (2016). *The good immigrant.* London: Unbound.

Tikly, L. (2020). *Education for sustainable development in the postcolonial world: towards a transformative agenda for Africa.* Oxford: Routledge.

Verma, A. (ed.) (2022). *Anti-racism in higher education: an action guide for change.* Bristol: Policy.

WA Thiong'o, N. (1986). *Decolonising the mind: the politics of language in African literature.* New York: James Currey.

Williams, P., Bath, S., Arday, J. and Lewis, C. (2019). *The broken pipeline: barriers to Black students accessing Research Council funding.* London: Leading Routes.

PART I

The 'weighted' waiting game: being Black and applying to do a PhD

Wayne A. Mitchell

In Part I, 'The "weighted" waiting game', we encounter the honest reflections of students starting the process of embarking on the PhD journey. For all students there are several considerations, ranging from making the decision to undertake doctoral studies, the process of finding the right institution and supervisory team, and then attempting to secure funding. As these chapters will attest, the current arrangements disadvantage Black students. They on average wait longer for interviews, wait longer for decisions, must knock on more doors than others to get advice, and wait longer to get accepted on programmes. We describe this process as the 'weighted waiting game'. In Sophie's chapter, as a curious young Black girl, stereotypical depictions of 'a scientist' failed to inspire her to imagine pursuing a PhD or a scientific career. Despite her academic ability, the rigorous entry procedure for an elite educational institution and the subsequent low admission rate of Black students served to reinforce the notion of not belonging in these spaces, invoking feelings of isolation, loneliness and self-doubt. The intersectional characteristics of being Black and a woman further underpin the feeling of being underrepresented and undervalued in her chosen field of Physics. This echoes the accounts of loneliness and sacrifice described in Nicola Rollock's 2019 exposition of 20 out of 25 Black female professors' career journeys and the strategies employed for surviving within the higher education system (Rollock, 2019). For Katty this 'weighted recognition' manifests in the 50 applications and three years wait before securing a funded PhD. The emotional toll of receiving multiple rejections with no clear reason causes her to ask 'Why am I doing this? Is it for the passion of the subject or to prove that I can?' This is mirrored in Sigourney's powerful chapter outlining a seemingly never-ending cycle of applications, interviews and rejections, which undoubtedly weighs heavily on her and countless others who experience this process. For Esther, despite her known desires to pursue a PhD, barriers in securing funded positions, and previously encountered microaggressions necessitated a period to recover from these traumatising experiences before she could realise her full potential in higher education (waiting to recover). The delays caused by institutional biases result in a weighted waiting time before commencement of doctoral studies. Similarly, Nina describes the impact of societal prejudices and discusses the struggles of a less than supportive and competitive grammar school system. These factors, coupled with being a mixed heritage person existing in predominantly White spaces while searching for their place and identity, exacerbate the onset of mental health issues. The journey to recovery proved pivotal in selecting her research field in mental health and the successful strategies employed for achieving her objectives.

Performative diversity in the form of widening participation initiatives do not consider the specific needs of those entering these institutionalised White spaces and leaves so many Black students disillusioned by their higher education experiences (Ahmed, 2012; Arbouin, 2018; Mitchell, 2020). A tale too often heard and reflected is the low continuation rates of Black British students compared to all other ethnic groups (OFS Annual Review, 2022). Sigourney's chapter questions the notion of equity, suggesting that the lack of transparency in the awarding of the final degree classification has consequences on future career aspiration (NUS, 2019; 2023). Her experience of multiple rejected applications is not uncommon for those wishing to pursue doctoral studies, however the blatant racial microaggressions manifested by peers and potential PhD supervisors towards Sigourney left her with the feelings of 'Do I belong in this environment?' For many, the continuing sense of a system that was not designed to cater for their needs stirs up feelings of isolation and a questioning of their rights to be in these spaces (Mitchell, 2018; 2020). In waiting for equity, we need to challenge the pernicious consequences of the 'awarding gap' on Black students, as the weighted degree awarding system is causing extended waits to the pursuing of their dreams compared to their non-Black peers.

These chapters highlight the impact and implications of the apparent bias, lack of knowledge and representations in academia for students from the Black community. Jason argues that 'ignorance is not bliss' and that, as a community, it is our collective responsibility to inform ourselves and not be reliant on others to provide information about PhDs. His work is a call for more role models, mentors, supporters and sponsors to ensure that the knowledge transfer is spread across the community to empower future generations. In paraphrasing Jason's view, it is for the Black community to *stop waiting for others to bring us information, we need to do it for ourselves*.

The varied journeys to PhD status show that not all routes are linear, and further emphasises the importance of intentionally reimagining and reshaping the pipeline to ensure that Black talent does not leak out of UK academia. The final two chapters in Part I confirm the importance of finding your 'tribe' and alliances, individuals and groups that recognise your value and actively work to promote your best interests (waiting for acceptance). Nina contrasts the impact on one's physical and mental health and educational wellbeing when surrounded by those who champion you compared to those that undermine and degrade you. Dwaynica demonstrates the importance of having role models, champions, allies, and sponsors who provide encouragement and positive affirmation. Despite not having secured a PhD place, Dwaynica's spirits are buoyed by the safe, supportive spaces offered by her 'tribes'. They provide the knowledge, encouragement and hope for achieving the dream of starting and successfully completing a groundbreaking interdisciplinary research project in her chosen field.

The road to PhD study is weighted against Black aspiring students. As you read their essays, critically consider, do the outcomes justify the wait?

References
Ahmed, S. (2012). *On being included: racism and diversity in institutional life*. Durham, NC: Duke University Press.

Arbouin, A. (2018). *Black British graduates untold stories*. London: UCL Institute of Education Press.

Mitchell, W.A. (2018). *Do I belong: challenges of inclusivity – a Black student's perspective* (unpublished work).

Mitchell, W.A. (2020). *Being an Imperial College student: a phenomenographic investigation into Black British students' 'sense of belonging' at Imperial College*. London: Imperial College.

NUS (2019). 'Black, Asian and minority ethnic student attainment at UK universities: #closingthegap'. https://www.universitiesuk.ac.uk/sites/default/files/field/downloads/2021-07/bame-student-attainment.pdf.

NUS (2023). 'Closing ethnicity degree awarding gaps: three years on #closingthegap'. | https://www.universitiesuk.ac.uk/sites/default/files/uploads/Reports/closing-the-gap-three-years-on.pdf (accessed December 2023).

OFS Annual Review (2022). 'A statistical overview of higher education in England'. https://www.officeforstudents.org.uk/publications/annual-review-2022/a-statistical-overview-of-higher-education-in-england/.

Rollock, N. (2019). *Staying power: the career experiences and strategies of UK Black female professors*. London: UCU.

1

Underrepresented and undervalued: my reflections on school, university and the doctoral application process

Sophie Martin

There was certainly a noticeable absence of Black women in science, let alone Physics, who had graduated and went on to do PhDs. The prospect of that one day being me had never crossed my mind. When I arrived at university, I came into contact with many different types of students, but few who looked like me. For some of them, going to university, and maybe even becoming a lecturer, was a childhood dream or something they had already envisaged for themselves. Perhaps they had aunties or uncles who had graduated and become doctors, or family members who worked in academia. If you had asked an eight-year-old me, however, 'What do you want to do when you're older?', I definitely would not have fathomed the idea of studying for a PhD.

That says a lot, given that I was an incredibly aspirational child growing up. My dreams ranged from wanting to be an author, to a food photographer, an athlete, architect or a graphic designer – the list goes on. I was the type of child who always wanted to try new things. But ultimately my dreams were limited by what I knew and saw around me. It speaks to the importance of representation and the effect it can have on what we perceive our potential futures to look like. Even if I had heard of doing a doctorate at that age, it probably would not have felt tangible, like it may have to others, because I had not seen people like me doing it. The image presented in books, films and TV is always of the 'mad scientist', with straight, white, spiky hair, big glasses and a lab coat; not someone that reminded me of my aunties, cousins or friends. Navigating that meant relying on self-motivation so that the inconceivable could one day become real – and that was ultimately the main thing that carried me through.

For me, school was a pleasant experience. I had positive feelings towards education throughout primary and secondary school. Growing up in a state school in London meant that I had friends and teachers with a mix of cultures, backgrounds and opinions. This continued even through to sixth form, which happened to be an extension from my school, meaning I had kept the same teachers and friends for most of my life. My entire educational experience had been packed with students of different ethnicities and backgrounds and I became accustomed to that. In my school, there were actually very few White English students. However, our different ethnicities were celebrated and united us rather than dividing us, and I expected the same beyond school too.

My decision to study Physics sort of fell into place; it was not something I had grown up around explicitly. I had recognised that I was quite good at maths, and was curious about things I did not know – so science was always a subject I enjoyed. By the time I got to A-level it made sense to me to study the subject that gave me the best opportunity to continue to find out more about our world and the mathematics that can be used to describe it. Physics had intersections with philosophy, art, history, finance, tech etc., so I could essentially do a bit of everything. So that was that – and all I had to do was choose a place to study it and continue on, right?

When I got to university, I was one of three Black students in my year, and being one of so few definitely affected my confidence. While I am glad to have grown up at a school that grounded me in many ways, university was a sudden eye-opener to everything I had been unaware of. It could not do anything about the systemic barriers that impacted my chances of getting into Oxbridge (of which there had been only three students from my school before me, as far as I knew) or the limited admissions test practice to better equip me. It could not prepare me for the reality of being one of so few, and having to deal with wondering whether the reason why people were not approaching me was because they did not want to. It was odd to think that I was potentially some peoples' first experience of speaking to someone Black. My rose-tinted perception of education meant that once I left the comforts of my school community, it was easy to feel alone.

I became more insecure of my ability at university. I found myself wondering whether I was always going to be at a disadvantage because I had not grown up reading Einstein from the age of seven. I also felt worried about fitting in, wondering who I had things in common with – I had not grown up going skiing annually or listening to indie rock. At times, I even feel insecure about my identity as a Black person – did my university change the way my friends from school saw me? When attention turned to racial issues, were people expecting me to speak up or to educate them? University was also a shock to the system because I had been used to teachers who knew me and had seen me grow up; they were now replaced by lecturers who would walk past me in the hallway and not even look me in the eye. Though I still managed to get through it, find a great group of people I felt accepted by and leave with a good degree, it changed me in ways I had not expected.

The first reference I remember about academia beyond undergraduate level was from jokes about the only science teacher in school who held a doctorate and made sure everyone knew it (turns out that person could soon be me). Even at university, I can recall being told not to apply to centres for doctoral training (CDTs) specifically because they were 'too competitive', and admission was unlikely without being on the dean's list or having a high first-class degree. There is a stigma surrounding PhD study that suggests it is exclusive to the elite. When applying, I had moments where I wondered whether I would be able to find a suitable supervisor – would they be comfortable around me and I around them? Would I stand out from my lab group and would I be able to make friends? It does not help that the application process requires references from senior staff members, many of whom I had never interacted closely with. I had been naïve to think that was the case for all students, since they tell you 'it's all about who you know'. However, it is also a difficult network to tap into when there is hardly anyone to identify with. For me, it probably helped that my CDT did not require me to have already found a principal investigator before applying; I could just apply as a candidate based on my experience. I think that gave me confidence, as I could remove any concerns about judgement as an individual and focus on my experiences and passions. Despite that, I still remember sitting across the interview table wondering if I would be more likely to get in as a 'token' minority student, and how much was actually down to my ability – a feeling often shared by my Black and minority ethnic peers.

If I had the chance to speak to my younger self, though, I would still encourage her to make the same decisions and choices. Now, having entered my final year, and already exceeded the expectations I had for myself, I have proven to myself that it can be done. There is also an undeniable sense of achievement, to know that I have defied the odds and succeeded in getting somewhere that others may have deemed to be not for me. Carrying that gives me pride and encouragement and, while doubts do occasionally arise, I have to remind myself that I am just as worthy of any position, goal or dream as anyone else in this world.

2

Climbing the rough side of the mountain: getting into a PhD programme

Katty Wadda

I knew I wanted to do a PhD when I was undergoing my undergraduate studies in Biomedical Science. From then on, I knew I wanted to be a research scientist. In my field, you are limited for chances in high positions without a doctoral degree, so it seemed like a no brainer to me. After my undergraduate degree I went on to pursue a master's and, on completing that, I decided to get a few months of work experience, while applying for PhD programmes. I started applying in 2017 and, by the time I had received offers, I had applied to almost 50 different projects over the course of three years. Now, I am a first-year Medical Science PhD student at a prestigious university, and the whole experience feels surreal.

There were many times I told myself that I was not going to continue applying and times when the thought of completing another application form would fill me with dread. Repeated rejections were a huge damper on my work and motivation to even pursue a PhD. I had convinced myself that I was not smart enough to be offered a PhD, which, of course, was not true. Some of the feedback I had received was that other candidates were stronger, or that I had a good knowledge of the project but my experience was lacking. Most times, I was told there were too many applicants to receive individual feedback. Even now that I have started, I am sometimes hit by a feeling of imposter syndrome when things do not work in my project or there are things I do not understand. The feeling of not being good enough to be in the programme still hits me.

During my many failed applications, I decided to continue gaining some work experience and train in my field of interest. Looking back, I am glad I had the chance to work and learn skills that have been extremely useful now that I am doing my PhD. One of the most important things I learned is that your journey is not going to be the same as everyone else's, and it may not go the way you plan it either. In some cases, it may end up even better than you could imagine.

The last programme I applied for I got into. It felt right to me the moment I saw the project. Love at first sight, if you will. The project itself was related to what I had been working on professionally. A lot of the programmes I applied to were just for an opportunity to do a PhD without much thought about my interests – another side-effect of the repeated rejections. I was starting to want the PhD more to prove that I could, while forgetting my original motivation. I think a huge difference between my previous rejections and when I eventually received my offer was my change in perspective. When I was applying for my previous programmes, I had lost track of why I wanted to do a PhD to begin with. Now that I am on the journey of this PhD, I am grateful for the reminder that I am also pursuing this journey for my personal growth, because I truly enjoy research and working in academia.

When I initially received my offer, I was very eager to get into the lab and start my project and, as a result, did not fully consider what the move back into academia and moving away from home would be like. Once I arrived in this new city, away from family and friends who had been so supportive during the highs and lows – from offering financial help, to pep talks and brunch celebrations – I was in an environment where I did not understand how the university collegiate system worked. I was also an ethnic minority and little things I never had to think about – like where to get my hair done or where I could find ingredients for dishes from home – were difficult.

I have no regrets about my choice; I am still very passionate about the project itself. However, I do think it would have been important to also research the environment before I accepted the offer. Sometimes, in the excitement of pursuing your dreams, you forget that your surroundings can play a huge role in your experience, and I wish I was better prepared for the transition from being home and moving away to a place that was as different from my home as one can get.

As for the PhD itself, I have just started and it is beautiful and challenging. There are a lot of restrictions, although very necessary, that are affecting the student experience. Doing a PhD during a pandemic has its pros (a lot more time to focus on the work) and cons, but the lack of a social life has made it a bit more difficult, I think.

I know the PhD will present new challenges as time goes on; however, I am very happy to have an incredible support system to help me through this. I have amazing academic supervisors, have made incredible friends and my family have been providing their virtual support regularly.

One of the best things to have happened to me was finding a tribe. It has been so refreshing and motivating to have a group of Black men and women who have gone through what I have experienced and more, and wish to break the cycle of Black researchers feeling like they do not belong. This tribe has shared invaluable advice, brought me into contact with incredible people, shared information that I wish I had access to when I was younger and generally made me want to contribute and invest my time into learning about Black researchers. I think that is something a lot of people have been missing and I am so glad to have found it.

I wish for every Black person in academia to find that as well.

3

What I wish I knew: deciding on when to pursue the PhD

Esther Osarfo-Mensah

I was 22 and feeling fed up, tired and alone.

The end of my integrated master's degree was fast approaching, and many of my White peers had already set into motion their PhD journeys. They were organising applications, reaching out to personal tutors for references, and moving into the world of research.

As for me, I could not follow my White peers; I knew that I needed a break. Despite wanting to also undertake a PhD, four years spent in predominantly White higher education institutions was stressful. I was acutely aware that I had barely encountered any Black academics. And, most tellingly, I had not come across any Black PhD students.

I needed to be back in an environment that permitted me to embrace my full self. Where I would not have people questioning the music I liked or the food I ate, attempting to touch my brand-new braids with unwashed hands, or spraying me with Lynx Africa for 'banter' and then being surprised at where l told them to insert the can instead.

Coming back home to London felt like a cool salve on a wound. Here I was able to find and eat as much Ghanaian food as I pleased, easily locate shops for afro hair, and be with plenty of people who looked just like me. I knew that, if I were to go back into academia, it would have to be here.

And the thing I was most grateful for was that I did not feel rushed.

In the final year of my studies, I was lucky to have briefly met a woman in her 40s who had just begun her PhD journey in the department. Our ten-minute chat sowed in me the realisation that it was okay to wait. To wait for a PhD opportunity based in a field I actually felt passionate about. To wait for a fully-funded position. To wait until I found a work environment that would positively encourage my development. But, most importantly of all, to wait until I felt more secure in myself.

I waited for five years.

During this time, I continued to work in Science, Technology, Engineering, and Mathematics (STEM), focusing on making science accessible to as many people as possible. Talking about science and its applications made my heart glow, and seeing the faces of children and adults alike, light up in amazement and interest, kept me going. But it also made me feel sad.

Part of my work also included encouraging budding scientists to study and work in STEM. I would do shows, workshops and activities singing the praises of STEM and how important it is in daily life. But part of me would also mourn the fact that I had not continued doing the type of discovery and research I enjoyed talking about so much. Knowing I had left science after having experienced a constant barrage of microaggressions that drowned my own excitement for STEM research, how could I encourage young people into these fields and possibly condemn them to a period of racial trauma too?

And then, one day, a chance encounter rekindled a tiny ember within me. I came across someone who was Black and was actually doing a PhD at my old university! My mind was blown. How were they surviving in that environment?!

After a conversation, they introduced me to Minorities in STEM, a community of postgraduate researchers mainly based in UK institutions. I felt like Dorothy entering the world of Oz. Suddenly I was seeing lots of non-White researchers, but, more importantly for me, I was seeing lots of Black researchers. And yes, things were not all rosy in their postgraduate journeys, but they had a space to talk about their experiences, and provide comfort and advice to one another. As a non-postgraduate student, I felt a bit of an interloper, but seeing this made me so happy. I could go back to my work knowing that, yes, doing a PhD is not easy – especially if you are a Black student in a place that refuses to support you in being your full self – but there are spaces beyond institutions that will help you.

It was at this point that it started to dawn on me. Maybe … *I could go back into academia*. This group had become my role models, they were doing scientific research – and thriving! They had other passions aside from science – and were thriving in those pursuits too! The tiny ember that gently smouldered inside me had begun to glow brighter. I opened up and spoke to more people about my thoughts about going back into science. I started to meet more people who looked like me through work, social media and at science festivals, all of whom were pursuing their PhDs. Each and every one of them encouraged me to just go for it.

Finally, a very good friend who was just completing her PhD told me about a doctorate programme she thought I would love. The more I read about it, the more I could see myself doing the work. I had finally come to the stage where I felt that I would be able to survive this new dive into academia.

I am so glad that I waited. Time away from academia allowed me to critically evaluate the experiences I had been through. It gave me the chance to understand the systemically racist structures that have been put in place and continue to perpetuate the restriction of Black people progressing and flourishing in STEM. Those five years allowed me to grow into and value myself, so that when the – unfortunately inevitable – racism reared its ugly head, I would see it for exactly what it was. And I would be safe in the knowledge that it had nothing to do with my worth, my right to be in these spaces, and my ability to do the work I love.

However old you are as you read this, I want you to know that it is not too late to start that PhD journey. Below I have listed five things I wish I had known when it came to deciding on when to pursue my PhD. I hope that these are useful for you too.

1. There are support networks out there

You are not alone in your field or in your skin. For me, spaces like Minorities in STEM, the West African Researchers Collective, and the Black in X movements, to name but a few, have been a wonderful source of support, advice and friends. Find the communities and talk to people who are already doing their PhDs. This might rekindle that ember inside you too.

2. Do not just jump into the first PhD opportunity that you come across

Really evaluate if this is going to be a space that will help you to grow into the person you want to be. Everyone says this, but seriously – talk to potential supervisors first and figure out if you want to work closely with this person and their research group for the next few years. My break from academia helped me to hone my intuition skills, and boy am I glad I listened to them.

3. It's okay if you can't remember 50 per cent, or even 100 per cent, of what you did in undergraduate studies or your master's

A PhD is not about knowing your textbooks inside out. It is about being excited about your topic, perpetually curious, and willing to push the boundaries of knowledge. One day, you could be contributing to those textbooks!

4. Your imposter syndrome probably isn't going to leave any time soon, so don't let it stop you from taking that leap of faith

Despite all the emotional growth I had had during my time away from academia, when I was accepted onto my PhD programme, I honestly thought it was a mistake. After responding, and receiving a second confirmation that it was true, I took the time to evaluate my feelings. If you let imposter syndrome dictate when you start each new venture, you will not do anything. So, when those feelings crop up, examine them to see how real they are. More times than not, they are lies and you are definitely amazing! (Now imagine a row of fire emojis in place of this sentence!)

5. Think about your motivations

Why are you doing the PhD? Who are you doing it for? What do you hope to get out of it in the end? Personally, I am doing it because, not only do I find my subject area really interesting, but I also hope that it can ultimately help to save lives. I am doing this for the young people I worked with. I am doing this for other Black people who feel, like I did, that it is not possible to return to academia after taking a long break. But, most of all, I am doing this for 22-year-old me, who had once felt fed up, tired, and alone. (Okay, I know that I will still feel fed up and tired in the next four years, because hey – this is the reality of a PhD – but thanks to the amazing friends and networks I have come across over the years, I certainly will not be feeling alone!)

4

The long and winding road: tackling barriers and prejudice on the journey to PhD study

Sigourney Bonner

I did not always want to do a PhD; it was certainly not on my radar as a secondary school student. Apart from two White male teachers, I did not know anyone else with a PhD, let alone anyone who looked like me who had done one. (It took ten years after leaving school to meet a Black woman with a PhD.) My initial plan was to be a medic. It was during my interview for medical school that I first experienced blatant prejudice in what was deemed a professional environment. After waiting for my interview and watching a consultant paediatrician introduce himself to other applicants as just that, when my name was called, I got up and this same paediatrician shook my hand and introduced himself as 'a child doctor'. I was mortified that he thought that I did not know what a paediatrician was. My mum was internally raging at the back of the waiting room and, afterwards, this resulted in a huge discussion between her and me about how to approach situations where this would inevitably happen again. Other decisions would lead me down another path and into research rather than medicine, but that experience, 13 years ago, is still clear as day in my memory.

My journey towards a PhD started six years before I managed to actually start on my programme. In 2012, I took a year out of my undergraduate degree to work for a pharmaceutical company.

Being one of two Black people in the department was not too hard as, by this point, I was used to navigating spaces where the majority of people did not look like me. I had been in the minority ever since I started school.

During my industrial placement year at the pharmaceutical company, I was encouraged to apply for PhD programmes, and I actually started to picture myself pursuing graduate school. On returning to university for my final year, after conversations with my lecturers and supervisors, I set about applying for PhDs. They were confident in my ability to gain a PhD position because of my level of experience and enthusiasm for research. After a few rejections from the programmes that I initially applied to, I was deflated but still convinced that it was the route I wanted to take. After securing an interview for a highly competitive position at a London university and being told that it went well, I ended up on the phone the next day being told that they had chosen another candidate, but the interviewers were not able to articulate why they had chosen that individual over me. Nonetheless, I carried on applying and this was certainly not the only challenging interview process I went through. Fast forward a few months and I had an interview at another highly rated university. I was told that I performed well in the interview and that I was down to the final three for two positions. The interviewer mentioned that they and the principal investigator (PI) just needed to meet one candidate in person before making a decision the following day. This was actually the last time I heard from the PI. They did not bother to inform me that they had not selected me for the position, and they gave no explanation or apology after I reached out to them to ask if they had made a decision.

After a number of rejections at a range of institutions for seemingly innocuous reasons, I received my degree classification for my undergraduate studies. I ended up being awarded an Upper Second-Class Honours, missing a First-Class Honours degree by 0.3 per cent because of 'low attendance' in the lab during my dissertation. This was a very strange outcome as my lab partner, who had attended the same number of sessions as me, had got a significantly higher grade. I would have easily obtained a First overall had I been awarded the same marks as my lab partner. The clear prejudice involved in the decision making concerning my grade for this part of my degree probably cost me a lot of time and contributed to the pain and heartache of rejections before finally being accepted for a PhD.

Those experiences led me to believe that my grade did not make me competitive enough for the PhD market. I thought that maybe if I got more lab experience then PIs would be able to see that I was both prepared and enthusiastic, and would grant me a position. I then went on to work at a major international pharmaceutical company, still being the only Black employee in my building. I continued to apply during this time and had a number of interviews. One in particular stood out and left me wondering whether I should stop applying altogether.

Again at one of the top institutions in the country, I had an interview for a project where I was the only applicant who had used the technology that the lab had developed – I had used it during my industrial year. I went to this interview with confidence, feeling like I had an edge over other candidates. I was soon brought right back down to earth with what felt like more than just a bump. It seemed surreal as, once again, I found myself in a waiting room and the head of department came in and called my name. Immediately, as I looked at him, I watched him roll his eyes as if he already knew that my interview would be a waste of his time. Irrespective, I put my best smile on and went into the interview room. Once the interview started, he asked me a barrage of questions that I managed to answer correctly, which he seemed less than pleased about. He then proceeded to ask me a question that I answered, and which was rapidly followed by a 'no' from him. I offered other suggestions for answers, to be met with the same response. Eventually when I gave in and said that I did not know, he told me the answer (which was the first thing I had said). None of the three other interviewers in the room said anything or backed me up. I left the room at the end of the interview heartbroken and demoralised, but not before he said 'well you won't be hearing from us but good luck'.

When I had managed to pick myself up and start applying again, I secured an interview at another institution, got to the department and sat in a room with the PI and the other candidates. We were then talked through the agenda for the day and they mentioned we would be giving presentations. I was the only candidate who had not been asked to prepare a presentation. I frantically took out my phone and looked through my emails. I was right – I had not been asked. I showed the emails to the PI and they simply said 'Oh, do you have anything you can do?'. I had an old presentation from a previous interview with me and they said 'Just do that then'. Again, like in so many interviews, I felt like I was to blame for being ill-prepared when, in fact, it had nothing to do with me. Needless to say, I was not offered the position.

Time and time again these experiences made me feel like I was not cut out for a PhD and led me to feel like I would never be able to pursue my dream. Alongside the lack of visibility of any Black women with PhDs, I then did not have anyone to talk to about my experiences and why I thought I was being rejected at the final stage for these PhD programmes. Eventually, five years after finishing my undergraduate degree, I ended up securing my current position, which was down to the project and a bit of serendipity in applying to a project based in the building I already worked in. I managed to build personal relationships with the group before my interview. I am not sure that I would have secured the position without this.

All in all, my road to my PhD took 17 applications, six interviews and five additional years of research experience. Many of my non-minority counterparts from my undergraduate degree have since completed their PhDs and are well into postdoctoral positions. However, even in this journey, I want to let other young Black STEM students know that if you want to get there you will. There is so much support available from our own communities. All of us have managed to open doors that we are working to keep open for those of you who want to join us. Your drive and your passion for your subject will bring you through. Reach out to those you see to ask advice – we all want to help you to achieve your PhD dreams!

5

Ignorance is not bliss: what every potential Black PhD science student needs to know

Jason Amartey

They say 'Knowledge is Power' and I think that is where we, the Black community, in general, lose a lot of power. Whether it is a lack of knowledge about available opportunities and roles, not knowing where to look or being unaware of who can point us in the right direction, we usually seem to be on the back foot. Many of us tend to be first-generation graduates and there is usually no template or an idea of which career path to follow, or at least that is what I have found in my experience. Within my circle, I have found myself sharing the limited information I have attained in order to help guide others. I have taken on this role almost as a duty, because I realise how valuable this information could be to others, just as it was for me. It is, however, when I sit down to reflect, a role that I also find extremely frustrating, particularly because I recognise how many opportunities there are for us, but we miss out on because we do not know about it. If we know what is out there and decide not to pursue them, then that is our choice, therefore a very different situation. In a way, it feels like we are always one step behind.

As I share my story, I will highlight some opportunities and experiences I was fortunate to have, that helped shape my decisions and subsequently led to where I am now. I will also touch on why I am irritated by the lack of awareness of what is common knowledge in a lot of communities, but not in ours.

I have always been interested in school; I was very comfortable academically and personally. I went to quite a diverse secondary school and although there were not many Black students, many ethnic minorities were represented. I specifically remember an Indian teaching assistant who used to look out for the Asian students, and me, and tried to make sure we stayed on the right path. She encouraged me to pursue higher education and would try to convince me that I was intelligent enough to take my studies even further than A-levels. Teenagers tend to be quite impressionable; therefore having someone who believed in me and my abilities gave me the confidence to believe I was capable of more than I thought.

I completed my A-levels then went to university, where I had what I had thought at the time to be a normal undergraduate experience; when I reflect on some of my memories, I realise this was not the case. One vivid memory is the surprise on some of our faces when a Black woman came to lecture us. I explicitly remember feeling shocked, with an immense sense of pride; I became quite fond of her and her lectures. I realise now how important it was for me to see a Black face in a position of 'power'. I had become so acclimatised to seeing other ethnicities represented in higher positions that when, on the rare occasion, a face resembling my own showed up, it seemed surreal. At the time, I was oblivious to the impact or significance of this, and it is only through hearing other people's stories that I noticed a pattern.

During my undergraduate degree, I undertook an internship in Malta. Though I enjoyed the experience, I knew it was not the career path for me. In the following year, I did an internship at a university in Turkey as part of the Erasmus programme. This was such an amazing opportunity; it really helped formulate an idea of the kind of career path I wished to embark on. I found the environment highly stimulating and knew I wanted to be in a role where I was part of a team of people who brought their individual areas of expertise together to work on a common goal. My experience in Turkey developed a strong sense of 'this is what I want to be doing as a career', which put me on the research journey, starting with a master's degree, then a job in research and, eventually, a PhD.

If anyone were to ask me for advice, I would recommend doing a wide variety of placements and internships as it gives you experiences that not only look favourable on your CV, but also help you to figure out what you want to do as a career. When I was finishing my master's and was applying for jobs, the interviews that I had focused mostly on my experiences outside of academia. I was seldom asked about my university modules and their respective grades. I was asked specific questions like 'Can you tell me about your time in Malta?' or 'What were you working on when you were in Turkey?'

These extracurricular activities definitely helped me to get to where I am today. I realise, however, that this is not an option for most people. Various academic, personal and financial pressures or responsibilities may mean that spending an entire summer doing an unpaid internship is not feasible. In my situation, it was not necessarily the most straightforward process, especially financially, but I had to make it work and the experiences seem to have paid off. My story demonstrates, firstly, the importance of being aware of these opportunities and, secondly, being offered support to be able to engage with them.

Deciding to do a PhD was mostly influenced by my master's programme; I had enjoyed the research environment and wanted to take it to the next level. I was extremely blessed to have a Nigerian postdoctoral researcher in my lab, who has become a mentor to me. He inspired me to believe that I had what it takes to do a PhD. The process of applying for PhD programmes was not easy; I received rejections with no feedback and would send emails to supervisors and not hear back. I was not receiving much support with the application process and I did not know what I was doing wrong. After a while of not getting anywhere. I decided to apply for jobs and to put the PhD dream on hold for a few years. I figured working for a while would widen my experiences and develop my skillset, which would lead to a better chance of being accepted. On my last day in the lab, before starting a job in industry, one of my supervisors, a professor, made me promise that I would do a PhD as I was too talented to not go further. He told me previously how, if he had the funding, he would recruit me to do it in his lab – but alas that was the end of the journey for now. Once again, it was other people's belief in me that motivated me to take things to the next level.

I ended up applying for a doctoral training programme and was successful. Finally, all those rejections and unanswered emails did not matter anymore. However, I did not know that I was heading into an environment where there were even fewer people like me. Academic institutions seem to have a poor record of creating an inclusive environment for all. For example, I was told a story about a supervisor who bought a bottle of champagne to celebrate their Muslim student passing their PhD – the student did not drink alcohol. The supervisor was quoted to have said: 'Since you can't drink this, I'll have it all to myself.' This may seem like a trivial issue, but is a perfect example of how academia does not always accommodate differences. It would have been more considerate to buy non-alcoholic drinks, so everyone felt included; but, as in many other situations, those in authority chose to not make an exception for others who are in minority groups. As a Black person, this is an issue I am all too familiar with. Instead of making changes to create an environment that is accommodating to everyone, institutions have often chosen to ignore key issues or been embarrassingly ineffective in their efforts to address them. The Black Lives Matter movement, which came about after the tragic death of George Floyd, forced many institutions to make statements promising change and to do better. This has led them to set up initiatives, funds, and programmes to recruit more Black students and staff and to improve their experiences. This is all well and good, but actually poses the question 'Why haven't you done this all along?'. Clearly, they have always had the resources to improve the experiences of their Black population, so it is unclear what was stopping them. This leads to us having to ponder if we are truly wanted in these spaces.

My journey in academia has demonstrated the importance of someone else believing in you. I feel lucky that I have had such people in my life but also sad about the countless people with a background similar to mine who have not had this opportunity.

I started this piece of writing by saying that knowledge is power. Many people in the Black community do not have access to appropriate knowledge and that is where I think the Black community loses a lot of power. There is so much untapped talent in our communities, and it would be a travesty and an injustice for it not to be enabled to flourish. For this to happen, I believe we need four things: role models to show that we too belong in these spaces; mentors to pass on the knowledge; supporters who believe in us; and sponsors to give us opportunities. If these things are done, the more likely it is that we will see equity in academia.

6

Being one of the few among the many: my journey to the PhD starting point

Nina Higson-Sweeney

At the point of writing this, I am just four months into my PhD journey. Fresh-faced and a bit wet behind the ears, I look to older students for advice about what to expect over the next three years. They warn that I have a steep learning curve ahead; that a PhD is a marathon, not a sprint, and that I need to pace myself if I want to successfully overcome the hurdles I will face. Their advice is important and valued, but what I do not say is that, as a Black student, this is not just a marathon: this is my life. I have been running this race since I entered the education system and, while pursuing this PhD may be the biggest challenge yet, it is not my first.

It is difficult to untangle my experiences of the PhD and the application process without first considering how I got here. Not only am I a Black woman of mixed ethnicity, but I have spent most of my life living and learning in predominantly White spaces. For a long time, I did not consciously consider the impact this had on me. In fact, I have spent a lot of my life actively avoiding thinking about my ethnicity, because I was desperate to fit in and be 'just like everyone else'. But as I have grown older and gained some distance from my childhood, I have been able to recognise that being one of the few among the many in educational settings has been detrimental – most significantly on my mental wellbeing.

Imagine this: you spend the first ten years of your life growing up in London. While you are not ignorant of racism (how can you be, when a friend says 'My family don't like people who look like you'), you attend a school where half your classmates identify as non-White. Race is present but it does not dominate, and you take this for granted. Your family then move to a small, seaside city in southern England, and you start at a new school. You go in on your first day without expectations, because school is just school, right? You walk into the classroom and are greeted by a sea of faces that look nothing like yours; not your dark skin, not your rotund nose, not your curly, kinky hair. Suddenly, race is staring you right in the face, and becomes an inescapable part of your reality.

For the next nine years, I was the only Black girl in any of my classes, and it was exhausting. My mental health rapidly deteriorated in my teens, in part due to the environment I was in. My days were filled with microaggressions: 'So you're half-caste?'; 'But where are you from really?'; 'You're not *Black* Black though'. I was bullied and it felt like a guessing game as to why I had been singled out. The fact that I was one of the only Black people in my school lingered in my subconscious, and I felt like, if I reacted in anger, I was playing into a stereotype of who they wanted me to be.

My mental health continued to get worse, and it started to have an impact on my education. In hindsight, I am not sure the majority of my teachers really knew what to do with me, or how to react or help, although there were a few who tried their best. I went to a grammar school, and it was much easier for staff to focus their attention on the White girls who were getting straight A*s rather than the one Black girl who frequently cried, left lessons, and struggled to grasp maths. I got to my lowest point during my GCSEs, and my therapist suggested that university was not for me. Being at a school that only valued academic attainment, this felt like the ultimate failure, and I struggled to see a way forward.

But things did improve. I stayed in therapy, completed my GCSEs, and left grammar school to attend college. While I still faced racism at college, it was more out of ignorance than malice, and being removed from an ultra-competitive environment did wonders for my mental wellbeing. This feeling continued to improve when I was accepted into my first-choice university and was able to escape my hometown and move back to a more diverse city. It is important to note here that I am a third-generation university student, and the support from my family in pursuing university was integral. At university I thrived, perhaps for the first time in my life. I still faced microaggressions (my White flatmate referred to everyone, me included, as 'his n*****', and told me I was overreacting by being offended), but there were more people ready to stand up to it, and I found that I was able to let down my guard, if only a little bit.

I give this preamble because my past experience is key to who I am today and why I decided to undertake a PhD. My negative experiences as a teenager gave me a focus and I entered my undergraduate degree keen to pursue a career in mental health. I wanted to be able to give back to the services that had made it possible for me to get to university, while also helping children and young people in a similar position. At the time, achieving this through a career in research was not an option – I assumed that research meant statistics and maths and, although I was in a better place both physically and mentally, it was hard to disregard the doubt sown in me during secondary school. However, during my third year I decided to do a placement year as a research assistant and it completely revolutionised my perception of research. Not only did it make me realise that I could do it, but that I could do it well. It was something I became increasingly passionate about, with encouragement from my placement supervisor. I kept in touch with her throughout the rest of my undergraduate degree and my master's, and she was the person I approached when I started to consider a PhD.

I cannot over-emphasise the importance she has had in my journey throughout higher education. After years of being shown that I was not good enough and that I did not matter, here was an academic who saw my potential and actively championed me and my work. She was a mentor and, importantly, an ally. She never presumed to know my experience, but was very clear in her openness to learn and to be available if I needed to talk. Together we developed an excellent working relationship built on trust, and I felt secure in the knowledge of her unwavering support if I were to pursue a PhD.

We had an informal meeting and agreed to put together a PhD application with her as my primary supervisor. In this way the decision about which institution I would attend was predetermined. But this worked out well because I lived nearby and had enjoyed my time at that institution during my placement year. I was aware that this choice meant attending a less diverse university, which I was slightly apprehensive about given my experience as a teenager. However, I think there is something to be said about developing resilience out of hardship. I would not wish my experience on anyone, but in the same breath I also would not change it. Academia is incredibly White and, although we are working to instigate change, this is a reality I will have to face throughout my career. I already know what it is like to be the only Black person in a sea of White people, and I choose to see this as an advantage.

My supervisor and I applied to as many funding opportunities as possible, including charities, research councils and the university itself. Unfortunately, COVID-19 meant that some opportunities fell through, while other recruitment processes changed. After several months, I was invited to attend a virtual interview with three senior members of staff. I prepared as much as I could by seeking advice from previous PhD students and exploring online forums for potential questions. My supervisor also helped by reviewing my answers and organising a colleague to conduct a mock interview with me, which proved fundamental. I ended up with two offers: one internal funding opportunity through the university, and one external opportunity through the Economic and Social Research Council. I accepted the offer from the research council and started my PhD four months later.

Overall, my journey to the PhD starting point has not been easy, but it became smoother once I found people who recognised my worth. If you are a non-Black academic reading this, I encourage you to actively think about how you are treating and supporting your Black students. Could you be doing more? Is there a way you can better encourage them and champion their work? Consider how you can use your privilege to be an active ally and help institutions develop into more inclusive and diverse environments.

7

Making the garments fit: transitions to a better place

Dwaynica Greaves

Being an academic was something I wanted to be before I understood what it fully meant. I knew that I loved learning and I felt at home within educational settings. As a child, my performance in school reflected this, but there was something else that was reflected too – my love for expression. I was always the child in parents' evening whose parents were told: 'She performs exceptionally in her classes, but she talks too much.' I laugh when I think about this because I now realise that, as well as an academic, I was a performing artist in the making. Social engagement for leisure was something I never sacrificed in early education, hence it is ironic that I now have a PhD place in Cognitive Neuroscience with a focus on social cognition and engagement. However, my initial inspirations did not come from a neuroscientific background; my interest in science stemmed from my love of performing arts, specifically theatre.

I stepped into secondary school with this love for theatre; however, it was there where I began to understand that the merging of science and arts was not straightforward. The curriculum prioritised 'core subjects' over 'creative subjects' and, therefore, having interdisciplinary subject interests as a high achieving student was not highly encouraged. I remember facing an immense conflict between the science and drama department's extracurricular clubs. It was then I knew that I would have to take the tailoring process of what I wanted my academic pathway to look like into my own hands because I did not want to sacrifice one field for the other.

One interesting factor to note as a Black student was that this conflict was not a racial one, as my drama and science teachers were all Black. I did not ponder this at the time. It was only upon recent reflection in conversations about early academia that I realised that my secondary school had good Black and Brown staff representation from the headteacher level down, and this diversity was seen across gender as well. Experiencing a diverse teaching staff was the norm for me but, of course, this pattern was not maintained in further or higher education. To me, it seemed (as sometimes one may not be aware of implicit or undercover biases) that my pressure did not come from being Black but more from being interdisciplinary.

I was excited for sixth form because, for the first time, I could choose all the subjects I wanted based on my career interests and skills. For example, one of my A-levels was in Psychology, and I was also able to complete a BTEC level 3 certificate in Acting. Hence, I was excited about going to university after, as I knew I wanted to combine Theatre and Psychology. However, I was hit with another interdisciplinary dilemma; the undergraduate programmes that combined Theatre and Drama were not accredited by the British Psychological Society. Subsequently, I decided to do a full Bachelor of Science (BSc) Psychology degree while pursuing my artistic interests outside university, which I succeeded in doing. Therefore, I would argue I made the right decision.

To cut straight to the point, compared to secondary school my university was not diverse regarding Black academic staff; so in that regard there was a lack. However, what I did gain was an introduction to the field of Neuroaesthetics, which would change my academic experience for the better and shape the researcher that I am today. I initially went towards my BSc with the career aim to be a drama therapist, as that was the only way I knew the field fused performing arts and psychology. Also, this path would satisfy my interest in therapeutic interventions and my passion for helping facilitate the wellbeing of others. However, being introduced to cognitive, social, behavioural, clinical and research modules birthed my interest in becoming a researcher, and I realised that I wanted to be a chartered psychologist instead of a drama therapist, researching cognition in a clinical or social direction. 'But what about theatre?!' I asked myself, as this pathway would then put me in a position where I would have to pursue my artistic interests on the side again.

This was a dilemma for me until I met my final-year project supervisor, who was an expert in sensorimotor and dance research. It was here I found a place to build a home in the field. This research is under the field of Neuroaesthetics, which is a novel field of research that merges disciplines such as biology, aesthetic science, philosophy, psychology, neuroscience and the arts to conduct research on the creative process and aesthetic perception, experience and judgements of art.

My supervisor's research inspired me to complete my first research project on 'The effects of mood induction on emotional perception of movement stimuli'. Here I conducted research that interpolated ballet and socio-cognition – I was finally doing performing arts and psychology in one project. Encouraged by my supervisor, I then continued to postgraduate studies to complete a Master of Science (MSc) degree in Psychology of the Arts, Neuroaesthetics and Creativity. The special thing about this programme was that it was new, and I was to become a member of the first cohort of graduates. Imagine that – a new programme that covers the specialised direction of the research you want to conduct being launched as soon as you finish your undergraduate degree – an actual dream! I was able to achieve my goal of continuing to conduct performing arts and socio-cognition research by completing a research project on theatre and socio-cognition entitled 'The effects of audience participation on audience engagement in theatrical performances'. This project was incredible because it was conducted in a theatre rather than laboratory, which contributed to the ground-breaking theatre research in Neuroaesthetics. Not only was I in a space that I considered my natural habitat, but I got to work with incredible researchers who I am now continuing to collaborate with. In addition to that, an unexpected bridge was built to transition me from my MSc to a PhD.

In 2020 I began the application process of gaining funding for my PhD research, 'Investigating the impact of theatre on social cognition and engagement', a combination of psychology, neuroscience and theatre, which brings my journey full circle. Unfortunately, I was unsuccessful with my funding but successful with gaining a place, which meant that I was in a position I described as 'academic limbo'. I was not disheartened as I was working in the performing arts and science-art field, so I was still in a place where I could build my interdisciplinary skills from an industry perspective; but I thought that, in relation to the PhD, my academic journey would pause here and resume in 2021. I was wrong. That same year a massive shift happened for me when I least expected it. I learnt the importance of community, specifically the importance of having a Black academic community.

In August 2020, 'Black In Neuro' was launched and, through networking via Twitter and attending their Zoom seminars, the academic fire within me was rekindled. Being surrounded by Black neuroscientists across the globe was the inspiration that I did not know I needed at the time. As well as that, one of the organisers reached out to me about a UK community called the 'African Caribbean Research Collective'. For me, this was the icing on the cake, as I am a Black British Caribbean woman, who is passionate about my Caribbean identity. Therefore, to now be in a research collective of Black British Caribbean PhD candidates was more confirmation to me that I should not be complacent about my PhD goals.

Through both organisations, I received so many international opportunities to speak about my BSc, MSc and proposed PhD research. Most importantly, the value I felt from both organisations helped me to own my period of limbo. I was reassured that, as a creative and academic, I was not an imposter; I had the right to be where I am. Also, both communities were a constant reminder that my Black Caribbean identity did not have to be compromised for academic success.

At the time of writing this, I am currently in a position of applying for PhD funding again, so my journey is not finished. However, compared to last year I am back with a stronger sense of direction, newly acquired skills and communities that I know will support my wellbeing as well as my academic progress. I do not know what the outcome will be. But one thing I do know is that I am where I need to be, in the field I need to be, connected to the right people. I have not finished making my garment, but it is already beautiful and, most importantly, it fits.

Reflections on Part I and prompts for action

Wayne A. Mitchell

> The 'weighted waiting' encountered by Black students in pursuit of a PhD are thankfully not insurmountable, as demonstrated in these accounts. However, unnecessary institutional barriers leave many Black students traumatised from their higher education experiences, making the idea of continuation in the system an anathema. Despite these realities, the determination and courage of these students are to be admired, but not followed. These accounts highlight the very real need for greater institutional support for the Black undergraduate community. What institutional support structures are needed to remove the current barriers? How can institutions provide better training and transparency in their admission processes? We should not have to wait. *Why are we waiting?* Starting the process at a disadvantage makes the next stage more difficult to navigate as the accounts in the next part will outline.

PART II

Being Black is not an optional luxury! Struggles for rights and recognition in the White academic space

Madina Wane

The following accounts present the struggles and barriers Black PhD students face in pursuing and creating novel research in spaces that are ill-equipped to support them. Each chapter is a unique story on how these barriers make Black students feel and how they navigate a system that currently disputes their rights and recognition of their identity.

Given the small number of Black scholars in UK academia, it is unsurprising that many students enter this space unfamiliar with the reality of the power structures and limited avenues for support. This lack of appropriate support and community in academic institutions can be isolating and clearly has an impact on the confidence and outcomes of many Black students. This is discussed in detail by Amira, who struggled with self-doubt during her studies. Black students in academia, like in other white-dominated systems, have reported adopting a performance, or censoring themselves to fit into the dominant culture. This coping strategy may, at times, allow them to navigate academia facing less hostility, but comes at the cost of reducing their sense of belonging and wellbeing in these spaces (Arday et al., 2021; Stoll et al., 2022).

Black students can also face a lack of academic support and investment in their areas of interest, which points to the inequitable research funding opportunities in the UK. Funding agencies and research institutions are key players in deciding which research projects are funded, which scholars are recruited, and what kind of infrastructure is available to support scholars. In Alanah's chapter, it is clear that despite Black students being highly motivated to conduct research, academic institutions can lack the expertise and networks necessary to support students' academic interests. This is not simply an issue of a lack of scholars, or lack of awareness given that universities make intentional decisions on who and what is included in curricula. In July 2023, the University of Chichester was criticised for making redundant the first British history professor of African heritage, Professor Hakim Adi (The Voice, 2023). The university additionally axed the History of Africa and the African Diaspora master's course, thus narrowing the options for students to specialise in this topic at postgraduate level. The lack of diversity and the Eurocentric focus of many university curricula have been shown to contribute to the marginalisation and lack of sense of belonging of Black, Asian and minority ethnic students (Arday et al., 2021).

Black people are not a monolith – our experiences vary considerably depending on our identities and how different systems of oppression 'intersect' within our lives (Crenshaw, 1989). The accounts in this section are reflective of this. In Hanna's chapter she explores the unique barriers international students face including: difficulty getting funding, no ability to raise concerns, and the threat of being reported to state immigration authorities. This highlights the importance of addressing factors beyond the education sector to tackle inequity in higher education. The UK's progressively anti-immigration state policies, such as the introduction of the 'hostile environment', has not only led to harmful impacts on students, but also to the co-option of higher education establishments (and other public bodies) as 'border agents', making the impact of these policies even more ingrained in students' day-to-day lives. Accounts from Black African international students reveal how harmful these policies can be to students' sense of belonging, wellbeing and engagement with their courses. It is also clear that invisibilisation and lack of understanding of these experiences remain within the sector (Zewolde, 2021).

In Amira's chapter she details how she has had to navigate the harmful stereotypes of the aggressive Black woman and, simultaneously, the passive Muslim woman. Young Black Muslim women in the UK have described the particular anti-Blackness,

Islamophobia and misogyny they face, and how much of a toll it takes to navigate this multi-layered discrimination (Nurein & Iqbal, 2021). How much more could students thrive without these compounding stressors and barriers? Understanding students' experiences through the concept of intersectionality makes it clear that we cannot expect a one-size-fits-all model to effectively address these barriers. Indeed, an inability to consider the varied experiences of Black students risks perpetuating the same isolation and marginalisation many are already facing.

Despite, and indeed because of, the significant challenges Black students face, there is a common thread of these same students actively resisting the systems that marginalise them and their peers. This manifests in more individual, internal ways through self-care, or in broader ways by directly confronting issues in their institutions. Hanna's chapter shows one approach to this: organising with other students to tackle bullying, discrimination and unequal resource distribution. Another approach is reflected in the research topics some students have pursued, focusing on the experiences and outcomes of Black and other minoritised people.

These chapters make it clear the kind of environment Black students face when entering UK academia. In pursuing their research, students are having to navigate environments that are actively hostile (within and beyond the university), where they can feel unable to be themselves, and where their knowledge and interests are seen as less valuable. Although there are important examples of support, success and belonging, without wider changes to structures, policies and cultures, the struggle for rights and recognition will continue to be the norm.

Four contributors were originally included in this section. The final chapter, 'The missing ones', is a space to recognise missing contributions. As you read this blank chapter, take a moment to reflect on the one and the many Black scholars who, for whatever reason associated with the machinations of doctoral study, have been airbrushed from the pages of academia.

References

Arday, J., Belluigi, D.Z. and Thomas, D. (2021). 'Attempting to break the chain: reimaging inclusive pedagogy and decolonising the curriculum within the academy', *Educational Philosophy and Theory*, 53(3), 298–313. DOI: 10.1080/00131857.2020.1773257.

Crenshaw, K. (1989). 'Demarginalizing the intersection of race and sex: a Black feminist critique of antidiscrimination doctrine, feminist theory and antiracist politics', *University of Chicago Legal Forum*, 1(8). http://chicagounbound.uchicago.edu/uclf/vol1989/iss1/8.

Nurein, S.A. and Iqbal, H. (2021). 'Identifying a space for young Black Muslim women in contemporary Britain', *Ethnicities*, 21(3), 433–53. https://doi.org/10.1177/14687968211001899.

Stoll, N., Yalipende, Y., Byrom, N.C., et al. (2022). 'Mental health and mental well-being of Black students at UK universities: a review and thematic synthesis', *BMJ Open*, 12:e050720. doi: 10.1136/bmjopen-2021-050720.

The Voice (2023). 'Prof hits back at uni moves to axe him', *The Voice*, 17 July https://www.voice-online.co.uk/news/uk-news/2023/07/17/prof-hits-back-at-uni-moves-to-axe-him/.

Zewolde, S. (2021). 'Racism and othering in international higher education: experiences of Black Africans in England', Working Paper no. 62, Centre for Global Higher Education, Department of Education, University of Oxford. https://www.researchcghe.org/perch/resources/publications/working-paper-62.pdf (accessed 21 September 2023).

8

Studying while Black: reflections on researching Blackness in White space

Alanah Mortlock

I will never forget the first time I read *Ain't I a Woman* by Audre Lorde. I was in the final year of a psychology bachelors' degree, reading outside the syllabus for an essay question I had written myself. Prior to this, I had thought of Black feminism as an activist term, but bell hooks introduced it to me as an academic one; I had not realised that talking about the lives of Black women was a 'proper' academic subject, and especially not doing so using a first-person voice. I fell in love. I remember going to speak to my then advisor about it – an affable social psychologist of identity with a love of George Herbert Mead – and him telling me he was unable to recommend any readings as he was unfamiliar with the subject area. I had a response, deeply personal and emotional, that I found difficult to understand at the time, but I recognise now as the stomach-turning vertigo of walking face first into the steep walls of academia's ivory tower. This was a moment of alienating clarity in a long history of those responsible for my education being under-equipped to support my development as a Black feminist academic. I think of this moment now as the start of a journey, one that I am still working out how to navigate – how to be a woman of colour producing Black feminist research in the White spaces of academia.

Years later I was confronted with another moment of dissociating clarity when I began to think in earnest about finding a PhD supervisor. Having loved the intellectual and political environment of my master's course, it was my goal to return to that department as a doctoral candidate and as the time came to prepare my application, I began to think about who I might approach as a potential supervisor. Knowing I was lucky to have close mentorship relationships with several faculty members, I felt confident beginning my search; until, that is, I realised none of their research biographies listed critical race theory – let alone Blackness – as a specialism. I faltered, feeling the tower creeping ever-so-slowly higher. Those of us lucky enough to receive advice about the PhD application process are often told we ought to seek a potential supervisor whose research interests closely mirror our own. So, in spite of my mentors' encouragement, I wavered in confidence. I began looking at other options, searching Sociology, Cultural and Media Studies, Gender departments across the UK for an academic with whose research profile I might more closely align. Though I found academics producing beautiful work on Black feminism, there was no-one in whose work I saw an intimate reflection of my own. Reaching across this gap to pursue a conversation about the potential of supervision felt paralysingly intimidating. I only applied to one programme in the end.

While I see the sense in seeking an advisor whose research interests closely match your own, if we interrogate the advice a little further, I think we find it is not as sensible as it seems.[1] This mode of thinking significantly curtails the kind of work – and ultimately the kind of academics – that can find a home in UK academia. Talking to one advisor about writing a PhD project on Blackness, I was told it would make more sense to look at US institutions. When thinking about canonical works of Black studies or Black feminism, I think many of us – and I include myself in this – think first of Black American traditions and theorists. This bias of perception renders the USA as the home of research on Blackness, and so the most fertile ground in which to nurture such work. But theorising Blackness is not singularly the pursuit of the USA and there is a proud sibling tradition of British Black feminism (not to mention others in Latin America, Africa, and across Europe). The suggestion that young academics working on Blackness would be best served by moving to the USA only further entrenches the cultural hegemony of Black American studies. The received wisdom that we must mirror the research interests of our supervisors closes the tower gates on young Black academics in the UK wishing to theorise their lives and communities.

Of all the excellent advice I was fortunate to receive while writing my application, I benefited most from this simple reminder: you will quickly become the expert in your field. It is easy to lose sight of this at the beginning of your PhD journey but, however similar your supervisor's research interests are to your own, it should not be long before you know more about your topic than they do. In the first term of my PhD my supervisor tasked me only to go out and read as widely about my topic as possible and, by the end of that term, I already felt enough in command of my bodies of literature that I did not feel I needed her guidance on reading lists. Following this, I have come to believe that there are far more important things than specific subject knowledge in the making of a good supervisory relationship.

My supervisor provides an excellent support system, perhaps not as a breathing archive of Black feminist theory, but in all things academic, professional and pastoral. I trust completely that she believes in the validity and importance of my project and in my ability to write it, so I willingly accept her critique. Though not always theoretically specific, her feedback is always thoughtful and incisive on form, argument, and the quality of my critical engagement. Her investment in my progress spans beyond my graduation thesis and she is happy to advise on unrelated writings, something I now know is not a given with supervisors. She is a font of knowledge on academic professional development and supports and encourages me to pursue external activities that will improve my employability. And, finally, she offers deeply practical yet sympathetic pastoral support; I feel comfortable talking openly with her about my mental health and particularly the toll the PhD takes on it. My supervisor works with me to help ease the strain. In all the online articles I read about finding a supervisor during my application panic, none of them mentioned how vital these things are in PhD life, but they are the things I find myself feeling grateful for after every supervision.

Of course, working with a supervisor who does not share my focus on Blackness does pose some challenges, further exasperated by being the only person in the department working on Blackness. We actually have no Black faculty members, or any other Black PhD students. I am mixed-race and light-skinned; being racially ambiguous makes existing in this space (as in so many others) much easier for me than it would be for most who identify with Blackness. But it aches sometimes, that hole where a community could be. I spent a lot of my first year feeling isolated, not socially (the camaraderie among my PhD cohort has actually been a real highlight) but intellectually. While I could put together my own reading lists, I had no idea how to go about identifying the most relevant conferences and professional networks, co-authoring papers, organising events. When my supervisor suggested planning a symposium with other students, I could not think who I might ask. At times it felt like I was the only one thinking about these questions.

But it is not true that we are alone; the academy's ivory walls work to hide us from ourselves and each other, but we are here. I went looking and found academic networks, research collectives and reading groups all dedicated to Black academics and Black studies. I reached out to PhD students from different departments within my institution working on Blackness and we formed our own support network. Yes, it took time and work that I sometimes resented having to put in, the extra work Black people have been putting in for countless years. But I found a community – a lifeline – and now I am in the department I believe my research belongs in, working with a supervisor who is supporting me through my journey, embedded in intellectual and professional networks I feel nourished by. This is the PhD life I wanted.

I have received a few emails from prospective PhD students – mostly Black women interested in Black feminism – asking about my department. They want to know how I find working there, if there are any faculty members working on Blackness. Whether I think they should apply. I encourage all of them. I never lie, of course. I explain there is not a Black feminist faculty member hiding anywhere, and that there are difficulties. But I tell them that their work belongs there, that they belong there. It is a sad truth of being a Black student in academia that our journey requires us to build the ladder as we are climbing. But we are here, and the community is growing.

Note

[1] Though I appreciate the degree of importance may differ by discipline, my own experience being in social sciences and humanities.

9

Through, around or over the gate? Navigating academia from a Black Muslim woman's perspective

Amira Samatar

For me and many others the art of poetry and storytelling is a vessel we are both connected to and lean on deeply. In reading the unapologetic stories and works of Toni Morrison, Audre Lorde, bell hooks and Dr Maya Angelou, their individual and collective offerings to the world have shaped so many of us. I am also from a nation of poets, so perhaps something ancestral lies in my relationship with storytelling. The truth is, I know no other way to share parts of my journey, parts of me, other than through stories and poems.

In this chapter, split into two parts, I will share pockets of my journey as a Black Muslim woman in higher education, beginning each section with a short original poem. Think of the poems as blinds that grant you access into the windows of my world. My deepest hope is that, in reading this essay, you are able to truly hear me and, in doing so, also have space to be heard. And that you are able to truly see me between my words, and in some way also feel seen.

Before you proceed, I kindly ask that you indulge me a little for one moment and take a deep breath. A real, full breath before you continue reading.

Thank you.

Masks

> You did the dance
> faked the smile
> hid the tears
> made someone comfortable enough to ask you a question
> And remembered to be grateful for the opportunity
> Well done.
> You can clock off for the day, I mean night now.
> Take a sip of water and leave.
> Just don't swallow all of your hope when the first bit of air hits your throat.
> You'll need that little piece if you want to come back tomorrow.

The 'performance' of who I was pretending to be in academic spaces did not come about overnight, nor did my awareness of it – rather as W.E.B. Du Bois (1987 [1903]) positioned it, my double-consciousness, the 'always looking at oneself through the eyes of others' was ever-present. I always knew that, in order to exist within the walls of the academy, I would have to morph into something other than the most authentic version of myself. What I am speaking of reaches beyond the standard self-editing we all do in various situations and contexts. This was more insidious, blurred by the Blackness of my skin and the silhouette of my hijab – this was something much deeper. I was a threat in these spaces, even at my most passive or timid, I still threatened the very foundations of White supremacy and empire that these institutions were built upon. I threatened the beating heart of Whiteness in its research, pedagogy and practices, I threatened the individuals and structures that benefit from the current order, I threatened it all just by being there. The explicit othering, anti-Blackness, anti-Muslimness, gatekeeping and daily 'caucasities' were all manifestations of me being a threat. But the reality is, I was the one being threatened, being threatened for daring to occupy space, threatened for speaking up for myself, threatened for reaching above my station.

We know how the weight of injustice largely falls on Black and Brown bodies, on the marginalised and underprivileged. As a first-generation student trying to navigate higher education, my immediate goal was to survive every module and deadline, every placement and supervision. Every time I walked through the campus doors, the goal was to walk back out in one piece. The material risks were too high for me; I had no safety net – this was it. I needed to survive this stage of my life – no ifs, ands or buts. I am not alone or unique in this experience; many other students racialised as Black and Brown also felt and feel the immense pressure of having no other choice but to survive in these spaces. And it is the ways in which we survive, the ways in which I survived, the strategies and mechanisms learned and adopted through trial and error that helped usher me along the academy's corridors step by step. It is within this basket of tools that I recognised the mask of performance I had come to assume.

I can only describe this mask of performance as a shadowed, vague version of who I really was, a more palatable vision and interface for the White gaze. I quietened my voice to not be accused of being the aggressive Black woman, but equally engaged in just enough conversation to not be indicted as the silenced Muslim woman. I disengaged from university politics and societies, from seeking to address obvious issues with racially minoritised students' experiences as well as the Eurocentric curricula. I disengaged from it all because I knew I would be labelled as the problematic one across the faculty, always complaining and having an attitude, the troublemaker – and that soon enough manufactured issues from the higher-ups in the department would begin falling at my feet. It is this kind of violence and risk that I could no longer tolerate. So I had no choice but to wear the mask of performance; to fake the smile and make others feel comfortable around me. But in doing so there was also a distinct price to pay – hope.

I began to lose hope in the system of higher education, that things could change for me and others, that the superficially ascribed values of equality, inclusion and fairness could actually be realised in these institutions one day. I became tired and disillusioned and, honestly, my confidence had hit a low. But that is the interesting thing about being a Black woman within these systems; you cannot help but feel that they were designed to destroy your spirit, to strip you of your joy, your sense of hope for something better. My faith, family and ancestors brought me too far to let this happen, I will not allow that to happen. After a long process of reigniting my strength and conviction, what I learnt to do was plot – not in a sinister or vengeful sense but to plot and plan my survival in higher education. I had to consciously plot and determine what I needed from the institution and where I could also give to communities and spaces where mutual interests lived. To plot on the day that the mask or front I was so used to leaning on as a form of protection and security would no longer be required or necessary. And to plot on thriving and not just surviving anymore. For Black students, showing up and coasting our way through university is not an option. Becoming hopeless is also not an option – we have to protect ourselves, build ourselves and plot our way through the academy to get what we need to move on to the next phases of our lives, whatever they may be. That is our job and those will be our journeys individually and collectively.

The doubt

> If you own it, it takes a piece of you.
> If you detach, then their words and actions will await you on your peaceful journey back.
> No no, ignorance is not your bliss, neither is apathy your luxury.
> Learn to filter instead. Strain out the fear and doubts.
> Rebuke the misogynoir.
> Spit out the taste of Whiteness.
> Shed the skin of their approval.
> And then break them.
> The matches they use to burn you.
> Break them.
> One by one.

My experience of remaining within the academy over a number of years has taught me several things and left me with a resounding sentiment that continues to ring loud and true; the longer you stay, the less you feel like you belong. This may seem counterintuitive, as natural assumptions might lead you to think that the longer you stay in a place, the more you would feel at home. If not, then the question begs, why stay in this place for so long? This is not simply a rhetorical question, but one indeed drawn from real-life interactions with several White academics and students who have so brazenly asked me this after I have shared experiences of what it is like to navigate higher education as a Black Muslim woman. To me the question 'If it's that bad why do you stay?' holds close ties to the infamous 'If you don't like it here, why don't you go back to where you came from?'. Sharing experiences of unbelonging, microaggressions and racism within academia during these interactions rapidly and unsurprisingly became a 'me' problem. The framing of this is not accidental, nor is it removed from the problematic narratives of exceptionalism often promoted in the academy through proximity to Whiteness. Such responses questioning why I continue to stay if it is that 'difficult' or 'painful' not only exhibit a deep lack of compassion and humanity but also a privileged commitment to misunderstanding the reality that so many minoritised and marginalised individuals face in these institutions. Enquiring about why I continue to 'stay', and thus the implication and suggestion that my leaving would solve the problems at the root of my experiences, certainly points to a denial of the racism and elitism stemming from the DNA of the academy. The obvious and undeserved response to such rhetorical statements is: 'Do I not have the right to educate myself? Do I not have the right to be in this space and succeed without being traumatised and othered in the process?'. Perhaps I am not *human* enough to be worthy of this in some eyes.

The personalising of racism serves numerous functions, and its ultimate goal is to disregard the root structural causes of racism and its manifestations and thus is intended to preserve its destructive impact. Another functionality of the personalising of racism, and indeed White supremacy, is gaslighting, is to be made to feel that any racism and bias I have experienced is merely coincidental and unfortunate. Furthermore, advocating for myself and others against such issues often leads to requests to retell and quantify lived experiences, which at worst results in being thrown into the dead-end of institutional bureaucracy, and at best is met with apologies and promises of change that seldom materialise. The desired outcome of gaslighting is the emergence of self-doubt and potentially even self-gaslighting in the face of this doubt and disenfranchisement. It is as though the system and its responses were designed to make us feel that way, to make me feel that way; powerless and tired in hopes that we/I might give up. And in that giving up, the evaporating of hope that occurs also takes with it any possibility of meaningful change. This is how the status quo is maintained and reproduced – how Whiteness is maintained and reproduced.

Ultimately, truth needs no justification and neither does mine or any other person's lived reality. Inequities in the retention, attainment, outcomes and employment of Black individuals at every level of the academy speaks for itself. A wealth of literature, research and recommendations already exist and continue to be developed. Despite this, substantial progression rarely arrives in a sector filled with institutions that are too preoccupied with patting themselves on the back for every half-action taken.

The only way I have managed to continue my journey in higher education is through investing my time and energy in individuals and spaces that align with my principles and values. Of course, this also extends to outside of the academy's walls and, truthfully, I have found this to be a continual process rather than a destination I have reached. Remaining grounded in who I am while also critically holding myself accountable to the beliefs I ascribe to have been fundamental to my survival in every aspect. Academia not only favours but encourages a culture of scarcity; that if you are not always trying to get into the next room and show others how remarkable you are, not only are you unwise but also inadequate. People may often conflate your boundaries with obstructions and your integrity and self-preservation with idealism and stubbornness but none of that truly holds water as long as you and I continue to never lose track of our 'why'.

End.

Reference

Du Bois, W.E.B. (1987 [1903]). 'Strivings of the Negro people', *The Atlantic*. https://www.theatlantic.com/magazine/archive/1897/08/strivings-of-the-negro-people/305446/ (accessed March 2021).

10

Fighting the power: challenging institutional discrimination – a personal perspective

Hanna Akalu

In this chapter I really grapple with how to challenge and confront institutional discrimination, while trying to use the processes and mechanisms of the same institution to obtain my PhD. Audre Lorde's words immediately spring to mind when I critically reflect on my experience: '*the master's tools will never dismantle the master's house*. They may allow us temporarily to beat him at his own game, but they will never enable us to bring about genuine change' (Lorde, 1984 (emphasis in original)).

When I embarked upon my PhD three years ago, I was full of hope and excitement to begin this new academic chapter. I had received a studentship to begin my doctoral studies at a small postgraduate campus based in London (with the larger main campus elsewhere in the UK). At the time, our campus had 14 PhD students, all of whom, except me, were international. Going into it, I expected the PhD journey to be an intellectually demanding, intensely challenging, yet rewarding labour of love. What I did not anticipate, however, was to find myself within an oppressive working environment, which operated through a culture of fear and intimidation and the systematic bullying of its marginalised PhD students.

Within the first year of my studies, I witnessed serious issues with the way international students were treated at my institution.

These ranged from students being denied access to work laptops, phones, office spaces, research training and, at times, being prevented from taking their legal entitlement to annual leave. These issues, while problematic and disruptive, were less severe in comparison to some of the major issues we faced, which included students being reported to their supervisors for raising issues about university practices, being threatened with being reported to immigration for taking leave, failing to process ethics form submissions, withholding information, and confidential emails being forwarded to other staff members. Outraged, I encouraged my PhD colleagues to raise issues through their supervisory teams and postgraduate researcher (PGR) representative (rep). However, as those further along in their studies explained, raising issues typically resulted in one of two things: being ignored or targeted victimisation. As I would witness, the impact of this victimisation was profound and had, unfortunately, already taken its toll on many students. Morale was incredibly low; some were unable to make sufficient progress with their studies; work was being disrupted and, due to the impact, some were seeking mental health services and undergoing counselling.

After this first eye-opening year, I realised that bullying and intimidation had been allowed to go unchecked for so long that these were now normalised practices in my institution. It also dawned on me that as the only 'home' student I had more privilege than my international colleagues – I could not be threatened with having my visa revoked, as some of them had been. As a result, I was less fearful of the consequences of challenging the oppression at my institution. Ironically, my PhD project aimed to empower marginalised groups through participatory methods and social justice research. However, I found myself unable to ignore the sheer hypocrisy of trying to centre the voices of oppressed groups, when inequalities toward marginalised students were occurring in front of my eyes. I began to question myself as a researcher: How would my work genuinely benefit marginalised communities when I was powerless to empower my colleagues facing similar forms of inequalities? To reconcile this dilemma, I decided to begin by confronting the oppression at my institution head on.

As part of this aim, I applied to become a PGR rep, as I believed this position would provide me with the leverage to advocate on behalf of PhD students and create change. At my first meeting as the PGR rep, my attempt to raise issues of inequality was immediately shut down with responses of 'we've heard this a hundred times before'. This response was dismissive and trivialised the severity of our problems, but also revealed that management and the graduate school were fully aware of the inequalities we were experiencing (and had been informed a hundred times by their own admission). This means they were willfully ignoring their public sector duty to eliminate unlawful discrimination and advance equality of opportunity. I quickly realised that I would need to change tactics and use their own tools against them. This included becoming familiar with my university's policies and guidelines to gain a comprehensive understanding of its duties toward us, as well as how they were breaching these. As part of this, I set up a new meeting structure for staff and PhD students that would be chaired by the PGR rep (me) and would enable PhD students to formally raise concerns and for staff to address these issues transparently. As the official 'spokesperson' for my PhD colleagues, this would provide them with a shield of anonymity, yet still allow us to bring these injustices to light. During the first meeting, I set the aims, which included addressing the needs of the PhD students at our campus and the ability of staff to meet those needs. Before the meeting, a dilemma we encountered was deciding which issues to raise and those we should leave out (for the time being). We decided we needed to tread carefully to avoid the inevitable gaslighting and denial of our experiences that the university was particularly skilled at, and that is a common occurrence when racialised communities call out institutional racism. Anything that could be potentially denied or excused, such as bullying, discrimination and victimisation, were not raised at this stage for this reason. We decided, instead, to focus on concrete examples of inequality and to take it one step at a time in our pursuit of social justice. This would be a marathon and not a sprint. I did, however, point out that the majority of PhD students were international. This meant that they were far away from their home countries, families, and support systems, so the PhD experience would be more isolating and challenging for them. As such, international students would need to know when and how they would be supported, as well as more equitable forms of emotional and practical support. Some of the staff found the issues we raised amusing, and displayed arrogance and indifference; others appeared worried they would be exposed and penalised for their failings; and some began to unravel and let their masks slip in front of other staff. By the end of the two-hour meeting, I had been shouted at by one staff member, who subsequently walked out of the meeting, and I was also accused of being 'aggressive' by a non-Black staff member (who was a person of colour). As Black women we are often labelled with this unoriginal stereotype, and our assertiveness and confidence is often conflated with 'aggression', or 'anger', and is met with hostility or resistance. If you ever find yourself in a similar situation, being branded the 'aggressive Black woman', remember that it is a calculated attempt to entice you to lose your cool, or to become more passive and non-threatening as they prefer us. In this instance, I maintained my calm composure and committed to finishing what we had started: holding the university fully accountable.

Following this and subsequent meetings with the graduate school and school board, there was a notable shift in the attitude toward us from staff within our department. They had finally realised we were demanding change and no longer accepting their tactics of fear and intimidation. One of our biggest wins arrived during a meeting with senior management, following a document we submitted outlining the more serious issues of inequalities and alienation, and its impact on our wellbeing. After a heated discussion with members of the committee, the chair (and ultimate decision maker) stated there was evidence of 'clear inequalities' at our campus. Following this admission, staff were no longer able to deny our experiences or continue to bully PhD students. They also seemed afraid of our power.

Feeling empowered, we decided to strike while the iron was hot and submit a joint formal complaint. I was warned by some staff not to go ahead with the complaint and that I should 'think about my academic reputation', which meant considering the consequences that raising a complaint would have on my ability to secure an academic job later on. As if there were not other factors that would reduce my likelihood of securing a permanent job within White academia! However, based on these warnings, I was concerned as to whether my institution, and those with power over my PhD progression, would try to sabotage this in some way. I considered it unlikely, as I had spent the past year carefully documenting the issues through formal processes (again using their own tools against them). While it was an intimidating and exhausting process, and a few PhD students later withdrew their names from the complaint, the rest of us pushed ahead with our battle. Following a thorough investigation, the university upheld several aspects of our complaint, though not all of them. However, after having been voiceless and demoralised for so long, this outcome was nothing short of a victory for us. Our determination and collective voices resulted in our experiences being validated and formally acknowledged as unacceptable.

Some of the smaller changes that followed included access to rooms and laptops, access to research training, and an MRes qualification that had, until then, only been available to those at the main campus. Another outcome was that senior management decided to adopt the meetings I had initiated and chaired as mandatory across all the other schools. However, a more important outcome was the exiting of the main staff member responsible for the bullying and victimisation of international students over many years. We celebrated this departure similar to how one would celebrate the end of a despot leader's political term – mixed feelings of relief, liberation and angst at whether their successor would prove any better. At the end of this year-long psychological warfare, the outcome of our collective efforts, which I pray provides hope to students facing similar injustices, resulted in an admission of failings, successful implementation of new procedures and processes, and a sense of empowerment among our PhD community. At last, a change had arrived.

Through this struggle, an important lesson I learned is that, while the master's tools will never fully dismantle the master's house, knowing the layout and structure of the master's house is still fundamental. Thus, when you enter the master's house, be observant and pay close attention to everything that is around you, because if and when it is time to take on the battle and the metaphorical match has been lit, you will be ready and fully prepared to go. The key to this is knowing their game, learning its rules, and acting accordingly – one militant step at a time. Part of our success inevitably involved taking the time to plan and strategise, rather than acting spontaneously or based on emotions – although we did release feelings of frustration privately. Ultimately, it takes a lot of courage, determination and collective strength to challenge a system that has been built on structural inequalities and institutional racism. However, if you do decide to challenge the academy, be prepared to be met with hostility, veiled threats and resistance, particularly from those who benefit most from our continued marginalisation, while shamelessly using us to serve diversity quotas. Having gone through this experience, like many others I became disillusioned with the institution and the performative allyship that it displayed while simultaneously excluding and targeting its racialised students. Yet, as I near the end of this journey, I remind myself that I started my PhD for an important reason: to do work that is meaningful and beneficial for historically oppressed groups, and I intend to fulfil this. Finally, as Black feminist and poet, Audre Lorde, pointed out: 'know that *survival is not an academic skill*. It is learning how to stand alone, unpopular and sometimes reviled' (Lorde, 1984; emphasis in original). Challenging those in positions of power is never going to be easy, but refusing to stay silent in the face of oppression and standing in solidarity with those who are more marginalised and intersectionally invisible than ourselves is absolutely worth the fight.

Reference

Lorde, A. (1984). S*ister outsider: essays and speeches*. Berkeley, CA: Crossing Press.

11
The missing ones

Reflections on Part II and prompts for action

Madina Wane

Academic research can help us tackle the problems facing our communities, build collaborations and resources, influence policies, and achieve personal development. So we must ask whose experiences, knowledge, and culture are included and valued in our academic programmes, and whose are not?

As Black scholars we are best placed to understand our experiences and, as the accounts in this part show, voicing these experiences can reveal possibilities for change and building community. What is needed to bring to light the experiences of Black students – what are the interpersonal interactions, platforms and practices that are needed within or beyond the academy?

These stories are immeasurably important but, without action, the barriers Black students face will never change. Think about who currently bears the burden of making this change and how this too contributes to inequity.

PART III

For us, by us: finding one another amid the storm

Jacqueline Darkwa

The collection of essays in this part speaks to the void created by the absence of established support networks existing within higher education institutions to empower and retain Black talent. This void has forced Black students and scholars to step in and create their own spaces of empowerment and encouragement. Black doctoral students, as seen in earlier essays, have already had to overcome great obstacles to reach the point of undertaking their research. Once they enter these hallowed halls they must now combat the experiences of isolation and segregation from both their academic peers and Black community – all against the backdrop of pursuing their passions.

It is hard to find a place where one has to undergo so much maltreatment for the simple pursuit of knowledge. Yet, as is expressed in most of the essays you are about to read, it is an inevitability as a Black person existing in academia.

Madina and De-Shaine's essays both speak to the experience of disillusionment at certain points in their educational journeys where they could no longer ignore the active discouragement and prejudicial treatment by senior White academics. It was this disillusionment that led them to seek out and create spaces where they could find community where there once was none.

The act of creating one's own community is a beautiful and often bittersweet circumstance. Beautiful, because there is nothing quite like being surrounded and empowered by a community of shared experiences; bittersweet, because this almost always comes at the cost of experiencing serious solitude and detachment. It has long been discoursed that individualism is not a native African ideology (Odimegwu, 2007). Take the African proverb 'it takes a village' as an example – widely used to impart the fact that community and togetherness are essential pillars of an effective society. This theme of community is seen in Paulette's essay, where she recounts how her mother's encouragement to maintain a connection to her culture and heritage was foundational to her starting the organisation Leading Routes. In his essay, Deyl highlights how a chance encounter at an Islamic Society meeting helped put him onto his path to pursue a PhD as a Somali-British student and provided him with a dedicated support network. But what does it feel like to not have that network? Mary's experience of navigating academia with the triple-edged sword of being a neurodiverse Black woman meant that her early years were significantly isolating, as seen in her interaction with a white female academic in her undergraduate studies. Her journey was made all the more complex by the ideological undercurrent that deifies the academic, turning them from a person simply driven by their curiosity of the world, into an infallible god.

Higher education is certainly not the only place where Black-led community organisations were founded in the fight against systemic oppression; they were an incomparable tool throughout the twentieth-century global civil rights movement. Sadly, in the twenty-first century systemic issues remain, but our tactics have evolved. In 2020, after the lynching of George Floyd and the subsequent #BlackLivesMatter movement, Black people around the world were galvanised in a way unseen in recent history. This is arguably in part due to the digital age in which we find ourselves, the time of social media where a hashtag acts as a flare to like-minded individuals. In Louisa's essay, she recounts the power of social media as a new tool in the fight for equity. The #BlackInTheIvory & #BlackInSTEM hashtags drew her closer to Black academics who have faced the same discrimination, subjugation and prejudice. As William denotes in his essay, in these spaces Black academics not only came together to support and empower one another back in 2020, but have continued this fight while others have retired their black squares. Through the dedicated sharing of stories and uplifting of one another, the community that we have been deprived of is coming together at last. It is the promise of a future where these communities and networks have done their works so effectively that we see ourselves and celebrate Black genius.

Reference

Odimegwu, I. (2007). *Perspectives on African communalism.* Bloomington, IN: Trafford Publishing.

12

That ain't it, so we'll create it: supporting Black students when and where our institutions fail

De-Shaine Murray

I am not the first and I certainly will not be the last Black trainee to become increasingly disillusioned with academia. To be wide-eyed and excited at the prospect of being stimulated intellectually, only to be challenged in every other aspect of life. Be it nepotism, unequal power dynamics, toxicity, abuse, racism or classism, just to name a few, there are a myriad of structural issues that need addressing within these spaces. Black students are often the most affected by these issues and UK and international academia are severely underprepared to tackle these problems. If institutions continue failing to address this holistically, the Black talent that is increasingly entering academia (with recent expanded recruitment efforts) will not be retained. This is ultimately a reflection of the unequal societies these institutions inhabit. There is so much work to be done.

I make such assertions after reflecting on my own lived experiences, navigating through the University of Birmingham, Imperial College London, the University of Cambridge and now Yale University. At each destination, I have seen the same patterns: isolated Black trainees, out-of-touch leadership, a gross miscalculation of the needs of the said students and an unwillingness to create meaningful change. Within these walls are the 'brightest minds' who undertake world-leading research and can understand, develop and articulate the most complex concepts. When those same minds are engaged to support the advancement of Black students, the results are more often than not unsatisfactory. *How is that even possible?* I have regularly asked myself this question, after innumerable meetings with senior leadership teams where I have left feeling perplexed, demotivated and upset. This has been because leaders will promise change but academic environments remain largely the same, with change occurring at a glacial pace, if at all. Unfortunately, this rate of change and amount of 'effort' is not sufficient to materially improve the prospects of Black PhD students. Nothing is being done to combat the screams from the walls that say we do not belong here or, upon observing the lack of Black postdoctoral researchers, the feeling that we cannot progress here, and, finally, when seeing the absence of Black faculty (0.6 per cent of UK professors are Black), perceiving that we will never make it to that level.

The writing is on the wall for people like me and this can be seen at all stages of higher education. My formative training was in chemistry at the University of Birmingham; there were five Black people in my year group. By the time I finished my degree four years later, I was the only one who obtained a master's degree and only two of us left with a degree qualification. I do not say this to highlight my success, but to ask what it was about that environment that was not conducive for Black student success. I know that there are greater challenges of representation in the physical sciences (a conversation for another day), but how are students, who have the same entrance grades as their peers, not making it through their degrees? At the undergraduate stage Black students are well represented (approximately 8 per cent) compared to their standing in the general population (4 per cent), but this more than halves for those who move onto master's and PhD programmes. There is a huge attainment gap that needs addressing at this stage, such that students can progress with the grades they need to occupy the research environments that follow, which are currently much less diverse. Witnessing this firsthand had a profound effect on me. When I later joined Imperial to undertake my PhD, I realised that my prior experiences were not an exception. At the CDT (centre for doctoral training) that

I joined, I was not only the sole Black trainee in my cohort but also in all five years of the programme! It was here that I began to understand my surroundings and take matters into my own hands. If the institutions that I frequented would not change, I would do what I could to positively affect change in my environment.

Unfortunately, this change can come at a cost. The burden of being a Black PhD student needs to be more universally understood. Whether we want to be or not, we are often elevated to being ambassadors for our race. As our numbers in these spaces are few, we often become representatives both for the institution, to promote its diversity, but also for our communities, to demystify the process and encourage recruitment. This is a pressure that takes its toll and I have seen countless Black students struggle under the weight of being overworked. Our peers often do not have to consider these things, and get to focus solely on their research, while we stay on top of our research and do 'academic housework', cleaning and preparing the institution for those who follow. I have struggled with this, trying to balance my PhD commitments while going into schools, giving talks and participating in outreach. I do not regret doing this – it is something I am passionate about – but the lack of recognition, institutional buy-in and support from supervisors and colleagues makes it much harder. This needs to change.

A turning point in such efforts for me was the publishing of Leading Routes' *The broken pipeline* report. It detailed that the UK's largest postgraduate funder, UK Research and Innovation (UKRI), awarded 245 (1.2 per cent) PhD studentships to Black students in three academic years (out of a possible 19,868 studentships) and only 30 of those 245 (0.15 per cent) were awarded to Black Caribbean students. Although the statistics were a dire indictment on the UKRI, the publishing of the report was a catalyst to the building of a national community. As a person of Jamaican heritage, I took exception to these statistics, and I began organising. On social media we identified students who were 'one of thirty' and created a group that eventually became the African-Caribbean Research Collective (ACRC). We consist of over 100 students and postdoctoral researchers across the country and provide peer support to each other. We also have a sister group, the West African Research Collective, that has a further

90 scholars. Although I have led this community, which has not always been easy, it has been a blessing for me and a vital support system that has helped me and many others find belonging and to successfully complete our PhDs.

Through this community I have learnt the power of collective organising. Much more can be achieved when the load is shared, and the importance of creating safe spaces for Black PhD students to just be cannot be understated. This is what attracted me to getting involved with founding the community that became Black In Neuro. I do not have to explain the turmoil in 2020 caused by the COVID-19 pandemic, but the subsequent 'racial reckoning' that we witnessed with the treatment of Christian Cooper and the murders of Ahmaud Arbery, Breonna Taylor and George Floyd led to a cascade of international community-building for Black academics. With a 22-strong team of organisers from the USA, Canada and the UK, we started a grassroots movement that has since become a non-profit organisation with over 800 members and a reach in over 60 countries. We support Black neuroscientists at all levels, providing visibility, resources and a supportive community. There are now 70+ Black In X groups, doing vital work in ensuring this generation of academics can thrive within the ivory tower if they choose to do so.

While undergoing that journey, I noticed that, at a local institutional level, there was still a void. I still felt isolated when our labs reopened and we returned to work. As a Black PhD student, you can go days or weeks without seeing fellow peers that look like you. I knew I was not the only Black PhD student at Imperial who felt this way, so I formed the Imperial College London Black Doctoral Network. This is a community that offers a space for Black Imperial PhD students to connect with each other. I hope this space will continue to exist and become a fixture of this university, and that such efforts are replicated at other institutions across the country, because there is a huge need.

The blueprint is simple – building organic communities at local, national and international levels that provide adequate, culturally competent support to Black students. These communities are vital, as they ensure that we are retained in academia and become the junior faculty and professors of tomorrow. If institutions cannot replicate such environments, they must, at the very least, empower and fully support the student organising that is required, be it financial, administrative or anything else, to alleviate the aforementioned burden. These communities exist because institutions are failing to meet the needs of Black PhD students, and the solution is not only to increase the number of Black students in the academy (as is currently being done) but also to create inclusive environments when Black students arrive that facilitate their future success. The ball is in your court.

13

Finding the Black immunologists in a pandemic

Madina Wane

Every two weeks, on a Saturday evening, I switch on my laptop, and join co-organisers from North America, West Africa and Europe to work on the non-profit organisation, Black In Immuno. Since its inception in 2020, we have created a platform to connect with, celebrate and support Black immunologists from across the world. Immunology is the study of the immune system, and understanding this system involves studying complex interactions, such as those between a virus and an infected cell, or between an antibody and its target. These fascinating interactions are what drew me towards the field of immunology, but it is also what motivates me to pour much of my spare time towards Black In Immuno. I am fueled to keep exploring and creating connections for Black scholars at the centre of this field. This need to build connections is very human, and for me it is rooted in the lack of Black scholars I have encountered in my educational journey.

The complex reasons for the underrepresentation of Black scholars were not something I understood during my undergraduate studies. I finished secondary school with no more than six other Black students in a year group of 200. This was not so different to the situation in my undergraduate course, where I was one of three Black students in a class of 150. I also saw very few Black researchers and faculty; however, this was not unusual for my educational experience. My prior years at school in south east England were largely absent of Black educators and I had grown accustomed to, although not entirely comfortable with, this reality. Although I saw little representation of Black scientists and educators at school, both my parents are university educated and trained in scientific disciplines. In fact, within my large extended family, my siblings and many of my cousins, aunts and uncles have been educated in the sciences. Being a Black scientist was, therefore, never something I doubted could be possible.

I did not understand it then, but the lack of Black scholars was the tip of the iceberg of the deep-rooted anti-Blackness permeating academia. Looking back, I saw signs of this before I even started my first degree. As a hopeful secondary school student with excellent grades, I decided to apply to several universities in the USA, drawn to the broader curriculum and fantastical images of international study and college life. Never mind that the $40,000 tuition fees were impossible for me to afford without a scholarship, or that most of these elite colleges had legacy admissions prioritising students whose parents were alumni. Still, I attended an interview for one of these universities, where an alumnus – now a senior academic at another prestigious UK university – was assigned as my interviewer.

I remember very little of the conversation except one stark moment. As a prospective student who had expressed interest in biological sciences, the interviewer guided the conversation to the topic of James Watson. Watson is a Noble prize-winning scientist most famously credited, along with Francis Crick, and increasingly with Rosalind Franklin, for the discovery of the structure of DNA. It was not until the interviewer mentioned it that I learnt he is also known (though less famously so) for being openly racist. More specifically, he has promoted the idea that Black people are intellectually inferior to White people. The interviewer asked how we should address the merits of someone's scientific work knowing they have done unethical things. I struggled to answer because, although I knew racism was wrong, I had also been raised in a world that celebrates people like Watson (despite their bigoted actions) and, truthfully, I did not want to sabotage my chances of a university offer. Was it a test to see how much I could ignore racism for the purpose of science, or a test of how well I could tackle complex societal questions? I felt uncomfortable at the time, but did not have the words to explain why. Over the years, I have gained clarity on why, in the context of the unequal power dynamics of a senior academic interviewing an 18-year-old student, this was a totally inappropriate question. Regardless of the interviewer's purpose, it is demeaning to use Watson's racism to assess the competency of the very people his racism targets. I bring up this story not to lament over one weird interview, but to show how, in academia, anti-Blackness is often seen as an inconvenience or peripheral topic of debate, rather than a major injustice.

In the end I attended a London university pursuing an undergraduate degree in Biochemistry and, later, a PhD in Infection and Immunology. Although I had a broadly positive experience during my studies, I was surrounded by the often-toxic cultures in academia: the rife bullying and harassment, the hyper-competitive attitudes, and the inadequate provision of mental health support. Moving from undergraduate to postgraduate studies, the drop in even the small number of Black people in these spaces was strikingly obvious. The promise I had grown up with, that Black scientists were inevitable, was left unfulfilled. It was clear that, on so many levels, institutions were failing to address these systemic issues, and thus failing their students and staff.

During my postgraduate studies, I felt more freedom to shape what I wanted to learn, both within and beyond my field of speciality. This was encouraged by my PhD supervisors, who were active in science outreach and diversity initiatives. I also started to connect with academic communities on social media, which expanded my network beyond the confines of my department and institution. Through these connections I learnt more deeply about the barriers facing many marginalised scientists, including bias in funding applications, inaccessibility of physical spaces, and the lack of recognition of scholarly contributions. It was disheartening to read statistics such as fewer than 0.1 per cent of professors in the UK were Black women, but I was motivated by a community of diverse scholars who were refusing to accept inequity as the status quo. By 2019 I had started participating in newly established Black science networks and was meeting more Black researchers than I had done in my entire education prior. So, when faced with the isolation of the COVID-19 pandemic and the constant news of brutal violence towards Black people in 2020, I dived headfirst into finding even more connections.

In some ways I was prepared – the need to find community had already led me to social media and, with the inability to meet people physically, it became crucial for forming and maintaining these connections. I put out a call on Twitter and quickly found other Black immunologists who had done the same. One online meeting later, Black In Immuno was formed. The major reason why Black In Immuno and other Black In X movements were founded in the first place is that, despite many Black scientists working and studying at well-resourced institutions, these same institutions do not provide the necessary infrastructure, culture and support needed for Black scientists to thrive. While Black In Immuno receives funding from many academic institutions, it is legally and structurally independent. Looking back, there was no real conversation about whether a new network for Black immunologists should be founded within a particular institution. As co-founders, I think we all knew that the institutions that perpetuated these problems would not be the singular answer to solving them. We were also focused on connecting with Black scientists across the world, and being independent of local and national institutions gave us more flexibility to broaden our reach.

Existing outside academic or corporate institutions means that we have been able to make decisions that do not fit with the way things are typically done. For example, we have adopted a policy of paying all speakers at our events, countering the norm of expecting free labour in academia. Black In Immuno is led by Black immunologists and, while we are supported by dedicated non-Black colleagues, we have always been explicit that those most harmed by anti-Blackness should be given priority in deciding how to tackle it. This community-led approach is both a source of joy but also an additional weight to carry as a Black scientist. Within our small group of volunteers we celebrate each others' successes, share career advice, and check in on each other during difficult times. Despite this, it takes an incredible number of weekend meetings, late night emails, and administrative labour to keep the organisation going. It is well-documented that Black and minoritised scholars face an extra 'tax', as they end up taking on more pastoral, social equity and mentoring work, compared to their White peers (Padilla, 1994). This work is undoubtedly important, but the fact that we do it unpaid, and at times unrewarded by our main professions, shows how far we have to go in making equity a priority in the research sector.

Ultimately, I do this work not because I think transformative, systemic change will happen immediately, but because it is a refuge from the inaction that surrounds me. This work sustains me, and I hope it will sustain our communities long enough to make more radical change possible.

Reference

Padilla, A.M. (1994). 'Ethnic minority scholars, research, and mentoring: current and future issues', *Educational Researcher*, 23(4), 24–7. JSTOR, https://www.jstor.org/stable/1176259 (accessed 30 September 2023).

14

In the meantime: creating change through community

Paulette Williams

My childhood was by no means perfect, but it was a safe and nurturing environment full to the brim with love and community. I have vivid memories of swinging on swivel chairs at the office of the Claudia Jones Organisation in Stoke Newington, where my mum dedicated time as a volunteer, and I later attended Saturday school. My understanding of my culture was nurtured by both the natural flow of life among family and friends, and the intentional efforts of my mum, who lovingly and purposefully guided me in finding a connection to our roots and traditions. Together, we took African dance classes, and she joined me in exploring and embracing my Dominican heritage through Kwéyòl (French Creole) lessons. I learned early on to value wisdom and knowing created and taught by people like me. These cherished experiences, among others, still resonate with me deeply, even decades later. As a new mother, I navigate these aspects of parenthood extremely aware of how meaningful spaces shaped my identity and sense of self. I have witnessed first-hand the transformative power of community.

Aspirations for me to go to university came from my mum. Neither of us imagined me not only attending but also forging a career in higher education. Reflecting on my early career, I often describe my attitude as 'ignorance on fire', without which I probably would have left higher education long ago. I was unaware of the magnitude of the Russell Group and its influence, lacked a clear understanding of postgraduate research, and remained oblivious to the entrenched notions of deficit that plagued my work in access and widening participation. What I believe grounded me during that time were the values instilled in me by my mum. Despite my naturally introverted and reserved nature, my deep pride in my Blackness and a genuine passion for my work gave me confidence. Over time, however, narratives across the sector surrounding raising aspirations for Black students and the depiction of the Black community being hard to reach began to bother me. This perception was in direct conflict with my upbringing and my personal experience of my community, and it made me uncomfortable. While I continue to explore and understand the multifaceted nature of exclusion and marginalisation within higher education and research culture, it was with the knowledge I possessed at that time that I embarked on my journey to start Leading Routes. Fast forward six years, and Leading Routes has grown into a small team of Black students and academics organising events and initiatives that provide support to our communities, reaching hundreds. Superficially, these events resembled those I delivered at my job at the university, just with more Black people. They provided similar information, advice and guidance; representatives from universities; and talks from experts. But as universities increased their targeted interventions with Black students, I realised that there was a notable distinction.

Feelings of isolation are common in higher education. Throughout history, academic institutions have celebrated and uplifted a select few, leaving everyone else on the outside. This is especially true for Black students and academics, who often face multiple layers of exclusion because our identities, ideologies, life experiences, and outward appearance do not align with the prevailing norms of these cultures. I remember having a conversation with my close friend, Dr Chantelle Lewis. We were considering what was missing in university provision. Chantelle was sharing her thoughts on bell hooks' work, and we discussed how institutions could demonstrate love and care. 'There are definitely people who care', I said, thinking about the many colleagues I had worked with who genuinely strive to improve students' experiences of education. 'But they're limited in what they can do. The university doesn't enable a *loving* kind of care. And of course, some people really just don't care enough.' Students can feel it too. They may not be able to put it into words, and they should not have to, but they can feel the lack of authenticity and the overall air of exclusivity that permeates the university environment. Universities are businesses that hold the dreams and aspirations of countless individuals, and they constantly struggle to strike a balance between these two functions. Even their attempts at inclusivity often maintain a strong sense of elitism. Whether it is undergraduate access initiatives that mirror degree programme selection criteria, staff resistance to changing meritocratic PhD requirements, or career promotion processes that heavily rely on social capital and networks, there is a palpable feeling that change is not truly welcome.

When universities ask about strategies to tackle racism, I often find myself uncertain about how to respond, as I am sceptical about their genuine receptiveness to hearing the truth. This scepticism comes, in part, from the realisation that they have asked because they have probably not engaged with the extensive body of scholarship on the topic, which raises doubts about the sincerity behind their question. Depending on the circumstance, and on better days, I might initiate a discussion about what it would require. Ultimately, for universities to genuinely confront and dismantle underlying structures of racism, they would inevitably need to question and reject the very systems of hierarchy, meritocracy and excellence that contribute to the prestigious academic rankings they possess or aspire to. It would demand a commitment to redefining success in research and academia beyond traditional metrics, and instead recognise the value and contributions of diverse perspectives and embrace a broader understanding of knowledge creation and impact.

At Leading Routes, we often use the phrase 'in the meantime' as a guiding principle in positioning ourselves within the sector. It encapsulates our recognition of the sector landscape and the substantial efforts necessary to bring about meaningful change. It also acknowledges the boundaries of our influence and frames the pragmatic approach we can take towards making a positive impact. Leading Routes, along with similar organisations, assume a crucial role in nurturing love and validation within a sector that presently lacks the capacity to do so. It is not something we always get right, but at the end of Leading Routes' events, people regularly approach me or a member of the team expressing sentiments along the lines of 'I needed this'. Being in a room of Black people where thoughts, discussions and expressions can flow freely, without the constraining weight of a predominantly White gaze, is like a long-awaited exhale, a collective sigh of relief. From concerned parents of participants on our Future Scholars programme, worried about the mental wellbeing of their teenagers during their transition to university, to prospective PhD candidates attending our Black in Academia events, who find themselves overwhelmed by the opaque application process, the spaces we provide are a metaphoric (and often literal) warm, heartfelt hug. The essence of what we strive to provide goes beyond simple information sharing and encouragement; it encompasses a profound sense of reassurance and solace found within the embrace of a supportive community.

Leading Routes has also become a sanctuary for me, offering a welcome escape from the intricate politics of my day job, where now (not so ignorant) I grapple with self-doubt and often feel the need to decipher the true meaning of interactions with colleagues. This lingering ambiguity prevents me from fully expressing my authentic self within the workplace and I have become comfortable with my more guarded persona. While there are many people – including my mum – who have played a significant role in the success of Leading Routes, my conversations with Yvonne Field, Dr Chantelle Lewis, Dr Michael Sulu, Professor Jason Arday, Comfort Moye, Jessica Oshodin and Dr Ayo Olatunji have taught me invaluable lessons about the spirit of community. These connections have shown me the beauty of intergenerational exchanges, the necessity of mutual respect, and the importance of transcending the boundaries of hierarchy.

Within Leading Routes, I have experienced community and friendships that continue to nourish and support me. For me, our relationships and our work reinforce the fact that change calls for a collective movement, where individuals assume many roles and bring unique contributions. We challenge notions of individualism and dispel the illusion of solitary heroes who single-handedly transform the world. We, as leaders and change makers, have in our own ways demonstrated the need for genuine unity and collaboration that goes beyond rhetoric. The same sentiment is present among the coalition of Black students who, supported by established Black academics including Dr William Ackah, collaborated to create this book. The group was formed following the publication of the 2019 Leading Routes' report, *The broken pipeline*, where we revealed that, over a three-year period, a mere 1.2 per cent of funded PhD studentships awarded by UKRI research councils were granted to Black students, with only 30 students being from Black Caribbean backgrounds. This stark statistic reverberated throughout the sector, compelling higher education institutions and research organisations to take notice, and prompting discussions on policy reform and the allocation of resources towards meaningful action. However, for me, one of the most momentous successes stemming from the report was the connection among several of the 30 Black Caribbean students on a quest to validate experiences and locate community outside of the predominately White academic environments in which they pursued their PhDs. This is the resolute power of Black solidarity that I grew up surrounded by. Grounded in mutual recognition and fuelled by a commitment to change. It is within this solidarity that our personal narratives converge and intertwine, birthing knowledge and influential communities, as we pave the way for our continued growth and progress.

15

Networks, networking and finding my place in the academic space

Deyl Djama

Applying for PhD programmes can be a daunting, difficult process. Having a support network – whether it is your current lab or friends doing PhDs – during the process is extremely helpful. I remember my first PhD application rejection; it hurt, but once I shared the news with my supervisor, he was very supportive and encouraged me to apply for other programmes. He advised me about the PhD application process and some of the realities of academia. As an undergraduate student at the time, I found my discussions with him highly valuable.

During this same time, at an Islamic Society 'meet and greet' social, I randomly met a fellow Somali who had just started a MRes-PhD programme at the same institution. We got along well, and he provided a more day-to-day description of what it is like to be a PhD student, and how applying for PhD programmes can be difficult if the support network is not present. Needless to say, he would inspire me and strengthen my resolve to pursue a PhD.

Through him I met an amazing group of other Somali PhD students and professionals, which has had a massive impact on my outlook towards the future of our community in the UK. As he told me stories about how other people landed offers for PhD programmes, it became apparent that who you know plays a big role, and that supervisors may have leftover funding or alternative funding to put together a PhD, which may not necessarily get traditionally advertised.

This made me aware of the importance of networks within academia, and that having good working relationships go a long way. My perspective on the PhD application process at the time was more rigid; I was more fixated on the formal application process, where the parties do not 'know' one another. Luckily, I had already developed a good working relationship with my supervisor and genuinely enjoyed the research and working with them.

I would see the power of networking during my master's year, where I ran into a supervisor collaborating with the previous group. We had a good chat and, by the end of our first meeting, he brought up the possibility of doing a PhD in his lab. It seemed too good to be true.

He introduced me to his group and my soon-to-be secondary supervisor. I had a chat with some of his students and they unanimously said that he was one of the best supervisors a PhD student could ask for, both pastorally and academically. My previous supervisor also encouraged me to accept the offer as he was a great person to work with, as well as a great academic. I still thought it was too good to be true.

I completed my master's project with him, which was a unique experience given the onset of the pandemic. But he was very supportive, and my project adapted to the novel mode of work. At this point the PhD was not a given as I still had to complete the necessary paperwork. But the main hurdle was crossed.

Now that I reflect on my journey so far navigating academia, I have been fairly fortunate to have met many genuine people who have positively enriched my experience and have given me many tips ranging from the things I should look out for within supervisors, to how to find my space within the academy.

To conclude, I shall summarise the key lessons that I have learnt so far from my journey within academia. It is important to build a good relationship with your supervisor(s), even at the undergraduate level. Do not be afraid to discuss career plans with them; they are usually supportive and can write some good letters of recommendations for you! Find a support network that understands your unique background. Little did I know that randomly meeting that new Somali MRes-PhD student would have such a significant and positive impact on my overall wellbeing within academia. Not only did he support me, but he also introduced me to a pool of other Somali students pursuing PhDs. This inspired me and furthered my motivation to pursue a PhD. This is why the work that the likes of the Black Scholarship Collective is doing is so important; it provides a platform for Black PhD students to share their stories and support one another in a somewhat underrepresented academy. It also helps pave the way for the next generation to pursue their dreams. Personally, without such a supportive network, I would be pursuing a different career.

16

#BlackInTheIvory: social media as a tool for racial healing

Louisa Brotherson

As a Black Caribbean PhD student in the field of Earth Sciences, I know too well the feeling of isolation within academia. Earth Sciences is one of the least diverse STEM subjects; in the UK, Black students represent 1.6 per cent of Geology postgraduate researchers, while 3.8 per cent of 18–24-year-olds are Black. This lack of representation has manifested itself in numerous ways over the years, from facing microaggressions from other students and faculty to piercing, obvious stares in rural Pembrokeshire on field trips. This feeling of isolation is a relatively recent addition to my emotional state if you consider my academic journey so far.

Growing up in the north-western suburbs of Birmingham, I had what many would call an idyllic upbringing. My secondary school was a diverse, all-girls' grammar school where I faced little racism. While grammar schools and the concept of selective schools themselves are problematic (overt prestige was one of the first lessons I learned there), I gained a rigorous work ethic, self-confidence, and lifelong friends. I was never taught by a Black teacher – in hindsight, this was perhaps a forewarning of my future academic path. However, I always had a strong, Black, academic role model in my mum. A maths teacher at a nearby school, she nurtured my mathematical talents more so than my own maths teacher, pushing me to achieve my GCSE Maths a year earlier than my classmates. My love of maths grew, alongside my passion for understanding the planet – Geography was always my favourite subject in school. Combining these subjects, I decided to pursue a degree in Geophysics, which is the study of the physical processes and properties of the Earth. Up until now, my educational experience had been relatively smooth, with plenty of Black peers who understood what it was to be a Black woman growing up as a minority in British society. Nevertheless, when I arrived at the University of Leeds, it was a shock.

Studying in Leeds from 2014 to 2018 opened my eyes to racism like I had never experienced before. I was one of the only Black people in my Earth Science department, staff included. Out of a year group of over 100 geoscience students, there was only one other Black British student. I was hyper-visible. A Black body in a White space. While I tried my best to blend in with my course mates, heading to the pub after lectures and taking an active role on the course, I stuck out like a sore thumb. During field trips, I was the Black girl whose helmet never fitted on her head because of the thick box braids that lay underneath. I was the Black girl who got ogled at by locals in a pub in Anglesey after a long day in the cold, wet rain. Microaggressions and explicitly racist comments followed me wherever I went, including in my department. For two years, I worked as an open day ambassador, introducing prospective students to our department. During one of these open days, a senior lecturer who had taught me that year said, referring to me obtaining a PhD position: 'You only need to add "disabled and gay" to "your list" and you tick all the boxes to get further.' This was in front of a group of about five others, consisting of students and staff members, yet no one said a word. I laughed along but, internally, I was mortified. This experience perpetuated the feeling that I did not belong in Earth Sciences. The suggestion that I gained my PhD position because of my race and gender was not only misogynoir, but was homophobic and ableist, and highlights how deeply-rooted prejudice and discrimination can be in academia – the career that I was pursuing further.

Fast forward to 2020, in the second year of my PhD at the University of Liverpool. My PhD project is dry lab and computer-based: I study earthquakes by generating tiny earthquake analogues under high pressures in the lab and measuring their properties by analysing the waves emitted. My new department was friendly but, like Leeds, very White; while there were a lot of international

PhD students, including several Black Africans, I was initially the only Black British PhD student. Nevertheless, I continued to do what I could to blend in, joining people for hikes (the countryside stares continued) and even trying climbing (not for me!). Although I had made plenty of friends, I felt increasingly isolated as the numbers of Black students kept dwindling as I progressed through academia. Day-in and day-out, I buried feelings of isolation and the microaggressions I faced deep within to cope in the academic environment. After almost six years in Earth Sciences and academia, I still did not feel that I belonged.

2020 was an exceptional year for many reasons: wildfires, Brexit preparations, the beginning of the COVID-19 global pandemic. However, the most important moment for me and many other Black people was the day that George Floyd was killed by police officers in Minneapolis, USA. The stratospheric resurgence of the Black Lives Matter movement protesting against acts of police brutality, where Black people including George, Breonna Taylor and countless others were unjustly killed, was emotively so powerful. Sitting at my desk at home, away from family and Black friends who truly understood the pain I felt watching all of this unfold, was unbearable. I felt completely powerless, beholden to feelings of grief and despair, as years of burying my Blackness to survive in White academic spaces came bubbling out of the surface. Trying to find solace, I logged onto social media but, instead, scrolled through endless black squares, triggering videos of acts of police brutality and performative statements from universities on how they always strive for equality, diversity, and inclusion. Everything felt so loud, my head rang from the noise. I stayed in this deep pit of isolation for days, until I saw the hashtag #BlackInTheIvory trending on Twitter.

#BlackInTheIvory was started by two Black women (Shardé Davis and Joy Melody Woods) who wanted to expose some of the racism they experienced as researchers in academia, the so-called 'ivory tower'. Candidly, they shared anecdotes of times when colleagues, students and universities themselves made them feel like they did not belong or had been openly hostile to them. As days went on, more and more Black researchers voiced their experiences through #BlackInTheIvory. The hashtag's virality led to over 5,000 tweets, each representing a Black person with a story to tell about their experience in academia. While their stories shocked some, they did not shock me. Instead, I felt empowered by their stories and was driven to speak up about the racism that I had faced since the age of 18. So, on Tuesday 9 June 2020, I sent a tweet that changed everything for me: I shared what the senior academic back at Leeds said to me, about ticking all the boxes. My story, of being a Black woman in Earth Sciences, was out. And it was cathartic. It felt like the heaviest weight had been lifted off my shoulders. Other Black people in academia reached out to me, stating that they had received similar comments. We stood in solidarity, finding comfort in our shared experiences and began to heal the racial trauma we had faced in the ivory tower of academia. Instead of feeling hyper-visible, I finally felt seen.

My #BlackintheIvory tweet reads: '#BlackInTheIvory is being told by a senior academic during my undergrad that as a Black woman, I just need to add "disabled and gay" to "my list" get further in STEM'.

This grassroots, viral movement, along with similar movements like Black Birders Week (31 May–5 June 2020) and #BlackAFinSTEM, inspired me to act and fight for change in my field. Seeing other fields create their own international movements on Twitter, such as neuroscience and chemistry, I searched and found my crowd: the Black in Geosciences Week committee, ranging from marine scientists to astronomers, climate scientists to other geophysicists. Together with this multidisciplinary team of Black scientists and allies, we aimed to create a global network of Black geoscientists by promoting visibility and opportunity through a week of virtual activities. After months of preparation, #BlackinGeoscienceWeek (6–12 September 2020) had arrived. Through panel discussions, viral Twitter threads and live academic talks, the week celebrated the richness and breadth of research carried out by Black geoscientists globally, while also highlighting the need for more inclusivity and equity in geosciences. The week was a success, with over 6.1 million Twitter impressions and a 3.2 per cent engagement rate with tweets. But the week superseded these statistics, creating international connections and representation in Earth Sciences that will outlast the event for years to come. Several follow up initiatives, such as Black in Marine Science and Unlearning Racism in Geoscience (URGE), have emanated from the week, allowing Black geoscientists to network with those in their research field and to continue to fight for lasting change.

On reflection, #BlackInTheIvory was a watershed moment for me. I discovered how important the feeling of belonging is in a system of Whiteness, such as academia, and that, through the power of internet virality, grassroots movements by Black activists can make a marked change. Racism in academia remains prevalent, but me and other Black researchers and allies are actively pursuing true diversity, representation, and retention for future Black students and academics. I no longer feel alone.

17

Unravelling the tapestry of unspoken rules: living with being different in the academic space

Mary Agyapong

Introduction

As a Black woman, I am not afforded the luxury of mediocrity. This is no different within the academic space, and is just one of the many unspoken rules that operate within academia. This essay explores my reflections on the time preceding my current support networks, existing networks of family and friends, and those that are virtual but no less valuable.

Background – undergraduate study

The current model of academia is unsustainable for anyone who deviates from the select few it was designed to benefit. This is particularly salient as a Black woman with a mental health disorder. It was never made clear that mental health issues were accounted for at undergraduate level and, therefore, how could I prove I was struggling with something when you could not visibly see my wounds?

I did not know I could ask for help, let alone how to. I will never forget the White academic who, with quintessential British politeness, asked me to never email her again after asking for clarification on my very first year-one assignment. These small interactions at university may seem insignificant, but in reality each experience was teaching me the boundaries of acceptability for me as a Black student.

Mental health services were incredibly inaccessible to the point that, when I had my first therapy session, I had already spiralled into suicidality. It hurts to recount the fact that I did not want to be alive. What is a degree if you are not around to receive it?

Master of none

Being diagnosed with anxiety in my master's year brought some clarity, but even more questions. I now had a name and a label for the chaos that consumed my mind. I was, however, already familiar with continuing regardless of what was going on, and this resulted in overworking myself – at times to the detriment of my health – to try and maintain standards of excellence.

The racism in academia is repackaged over and over again; there is nothing new under the sun. This is not only a biblical concept but something that deeply resonates with me, which is so well articulated by James Baldwin's statement on institutions: 'I don't know what most white people in this country feel, but I can only conclude what they feel from the state of their institutions' (Baldwin, 1969). I have observed every hour in the circadian, working tirelessly for the ivory tower in the blueish hues of dawn, and the pink-orange hues of summer's dusk. Yet the pressure of overworking in every light of day only echoes the pressures of academia – which barely uses its working hours to protect me and my Blackness. The constant feeling that something is inherently wrong with me, and overcompensating for this in my work, is exacerbated by academia's unsustainable work culture. My anxious brain takes that as confirmation that I should not be here. This cycle has taught me what academia values. Yet from the sun's rising to its setting I have an assurance of God's presence – an important personal constant in this journey.

It will not come as a surprise that I was the only Black student on my MSc course. The reality of this weighed so heavily on me that I almost dropped out many times throughout the year. I have also had people allude that I must have been a diversity admission – because the funding process was so competitive, I could not possibly have been admitted on my merits. I also remember saying to a friend that, in addition to there being no Black people on my course, why was everyone White in the participants section? Why was nobody of African ancestry in the genetics studies we read? Despite my criticisms, nobody addressed the elephant in the room. It dawned on me they could not even see it, and did not think about it.

As a result, I attempted the first few assignments without any assistance, almost to prove the doubters wrong. I had never finished an exam at university – the first time I achieved this feat was the last set of written exams in my MSc, which were also the first where I had been given extended time due to my anxiety. I was so relieved at the opportunity to have had a fair shot at each question in the exam that, for once, I did not care about the outcome. It felt liberating! I had never been able to leave with a quiet confidence of success; instead, I was distraught, with an overwhelming sense of failure, which was so often false. But I could not see it, I cannot see it because anxiety is the lens I cannot remove. This is why it is imperative to have those around you that reaffirm who you are, and remind you when you cannot do this for yourself.

Friends and family

One major challenge, as the first in the family to pursue postgraduate education, is that some of my biggest supporters have no idea what I *really* do. I was born and raised in London by Ghanaian parents, who have always emphasised the importance of education. Over the years, my parents have encouraged me and my siblings to pursue what they were not given the opportunity to. My family would call me a 'postgraduate' long before I was old enough to know what the word meant. But the real beauty of these relationships is that their support for me in my pursuit of academia is secondary to their support for me as a person, regardless of what I do.

Only a few friends knew about my anxiety. Being Black in academia also makes you a master of being inconspicuous, alternating between hypervisibility and invisibility in any given circumstance. Despite this, I knew I wanted to undertake further study. I only applied to funded programmes as I would not have been able to afford it otherwise. I had initially written myself off, but then a good friend said: 'You could apply for a funded master's.' I thought: 'So you're trying to tell me that someone will pay for *me* to study?'

I was discouraged by White academics on multiple occasions, who told me it was too hard, while with the same breath were supporting my White counterparts. Yet there were a few who believed in me and supported my application. However, getting onto a postgraduate course is one thing. Surviving – and trying to thrive – is another.

West African Research Collective

Unfortunately, I am used to being the only Black person in my research team. This is the status quo in academia and, if not the only, we are always one of few. I was also the only Black student on my master's course and the first time I've ever had a Black teacher or lecturer was during my master's. What I already knew from experience was affirmed by the 2019 Leading Routes' *The broken pipeline* report, showing that, out of 19,868 students, a mere 1.2 per cent of Black students were funded over a three-year period. I am one of the 1.2 per cent.

It is a striking figure and reiterates that no amount of degrees can distract from the fact that I am Black, and navigate academia and my campus in my Blackness. Research can feel quite lonely at times, especially when you do not see yourself reflected in your surroundings day to day.

The first time I joined an African-Caribbean Research Collective (ACRC) meeting was my first time being in an academic space where I felt like I could unfold, fresh with the weight of the resurgence of the Black Lives Matter movement following the murder of George Floyd and Breonna Taylor (and the global protests that followed). Nobody in my research team uttered a word about it. It became clear that Black people were living in a different reality. I was barely functioning, overwhelmed with sorrow, confusion and anger. Yet in this space ACRC my shoulders physically dropped and I could breathe slowly again. I felt comforted by not being the only Black face in the room/rectangle on Zoom.

Oumie Kuyateh and I decided we needed more spaces like this, and knew there must be others like us. That is how the West African Research Collective was born. We took the initiative and created a new space where, as with the ACRC (our sister group), we enter into a research collective with some common ground – a safe space, sense of belonging, community and empowering each other as Black PhD and Early Career researchers. There is something special about not having to preface your statements with explanations. A space where I could just be. Place and space to unfold (physically and mentally) is which invaluable.

My virtual reality

Social media (specifically Twitter) is a paradoxical virtual space. Curating my timeline to follow people I want to see and hear from means I get a nice balance of Black Twitter, Academic/Science Twitter, and some content from Black creatives. However, sometimes it can feel very intense – Twitter almost *always* hears things first, and things have a lifespan of about 48 hours. It can be overwhelming trying to keep up. It is not fun to try and filter through what is and is not 'real' – it can be hard enough doing that with in-person interactions. Social media is not always the kindest of spaces either – and my anxious brain often wonders if anyone cares about what I have to say.

Needless to say, when the COVID-19 pandemic hit, like many people I struggled to adapt to the new entirely virtual way of life. Yet in many ways the pandemic was the catalyst that pushed me out of my comfort zone when it came to making friends and networking online. For the first time, I found myself having more meaningful engagement with people I had never met 'in real life'. Reading the stories others were brave enough to share on #BlackInTheIvory, it felt like someone had published a long list of my own experiences.

After a viral video of Christian Cooper shook me while I was already feeling quite fragile, I became aware of a number of Black in X movements emerging on the timeline. I supported and engaged with content from a few different weeks, such as Black Birders Week, Black in Mental Health, and Black in Geosciences; but the movement that I felt most aligned with (and still do to this day) was Black in Neuro.

Black in Neuro is a global network for Black people in neuroscience fields. The network began with Black in Neuro Week in the midst of 2020, which was a difficult year to be a Black person. They organised a week of panel talks, a journal club, networking events and more. Furthermore, they created a website that hosts the profiles of anyone who is part of the network. I have personally had various opportunities that have stemmed from people seeing my profile on the website.

I have made friends through Black in Neuro social events. And through professional development events, I have also been equipped with skills that will help me in my academic career, in a space that is tailored to me as a Black academic. I will always be grateful that the Black in Neuro team persevered to make Black in Neuro Week happen, and they continue to support my personal and professional development. It did not matter that we had never met each other in person; we were united in our academic interests and our Blackness, navigating the shocks and waves of 2020 together.

Conclusion

In summary, it is wholly inefficient for you to be your own support system during postgraduate study. You need the help of a community to encourage you and remind you of who you are when you need it most. It is a true blessing to have supportive friends and family. But sometimes support and solidarity form in abundance where you least expect. It can feel scary at first. Do not be afraid to lean in and allow yourself to unfold, to support and be supported. That is where you will start to thrive.

References

Baldwin, J. (1969). 'Interviewed by Paul Weiss', *The Dick Cavett Show*, 16 May. https://www.youtube.com/watch?v=hzH5IDnL aBA&ab_channel=TheDickCavettShow.

Williams, P., Bath, S., Arday, J. and Lewis, C. (2019). *The broken pipeline: barriers to Black students accessing Research Council funding*. London: Leading Routes.

18

Making space for Black voices and Black visions: the formation and work of the African Diaspora Postgraduate Network

William Ackah

When I was an undergraduate student at university in the mid-1980s I often found myself being the only Black person in the midst of a sea of White faces at lectures. Having been brought up and raised in London surrounded by people from a wide range of cultural and ethnic backgrounds, it was very unnerving to inhabit a space of learning where I was a minority of one. In such an environment I was constantly second-guessing myself as to what to think, what to write, how to behave and how to relate to the people and processes that I believed would determine my academic destiny. Fast forward to the 2000s, I had successfully managed to navigate through undergraduate and postgraduate systems of learning and was now teaching and researching in a university. At the undergraduate level where I taught there existed large numbers of Black students, but at postgraduate level, especially at doctoral level, I was continually encountering isolated Black individual students, who were second-guessing themselves and suffering just as I was so many years ago. We were, and are as academics and higher-level students, existing in institutional spaces that regarded Black intellectual endeavour as marginal to the life and work of the university. It is out of this context that the African Diaspora Postgraduate Network (ADPN) was born and continues to operate. In this portrait I will outline how it was formed, the work it has undertaken, its impact and what its continuing existence reveals about the state of doctoral study in British universities today.

It was in 2012 that Professor Robert Beckford came up with the proposal that he and I, as two Black academics based in higher education institutions, should create a space for our respective doctoral students to come together in a supportive Black-led environment. He was based in Canterbury, Kent in the south of England at the time, but the overwhelming majority of his Black doctoral students were based in and around London and found the Canterbury academic environment very isolating. I was based in London and had access to classroom space, and so we came together. The African Diaspora Religion and Culture Network as it was originally named was conceptualised as a space where Black students could learn from Black academics and each other about how to complete a PhD. A crucial element of our convening was that they could learn to do this while staying true to their Black sense of identity and personhood. We consciously aimed to provide our students with a nurturing environment where they could test out their ideas and freely develop their consciousness as emerging Black intellectuals. We utilised the space to provide students with the latest thinking in Black academic thought, the literature and methods that could be utilised to advance Black scholarship and tips and strategies for getting through every stage of the doctoral processes from admission to completion. We were fortunate to have access to Black academic networks in the USA and the UK, including the important foundational work undertaken by Monique Charles and Antoinette Kwegan of the Black Doctoral UK network.

Professor Beckford and I volunteered our time to support the students, and once a month on a Thursday the London International Development Centre became our home away from home. Initially it was only our own students that came to the meetings but, by word of mouth, news spread that there was a Black-led group discussing religion, politics and culture. So other students came along; friends and family members of students also joined. In the spirit of ubuntu we recognised that it takes a village to produce a Black intellectual; so we welcomed everyone with a need or a listening and learning ear to come. We did not turn people away, even when our small room was at capacity.

In 2018–19 Professor Beckford left his position in Canterbury and could no longer support the network on a full-time basis. As a result, I held discussions with Paulette Williams, the director of Leading Routes: Black in Academia. She, Chantelle Lewis and their team had been engaging in ground-breaking work promoting the needs of Black postgraduate students in the UK and highlighting opportunities and pathways for Black students from school to university. We agreed to partner together, and Dr Gabriella Beckles-Raymond, who had previously worked in Canterbury and played a leading role in supporting the network, became the co-leader of the network alongside me. With Leading Routes now recruiting students for us, we renamed the network the African Diaspora Postgraduate Network and opened up the space to current and prospective PhD students across London studying humanities or social sciences. We had hoped to recruit a core group of 20–30 students, but had triple that number declaring an interest. Due to the new partnership, we also decided to engage more directly with my institution Birkbeck, University of London; and so they now provided the space for us to meet. To our surprise we regularly had students attend from as far afield as Birmingham in the Midlands and from institutions across the country. When the pandemic hit, we moved the programme online, and that has resulted in doctoral students from the USA joining alongside UK counterparts.

An extraordinarily inspiring feature of the network has been to hear the sheer range of Black genius that is in existence in UK doctoral study – from sociology to psychology, media and film, to music, arts, health, education, international development, history and on and on. Black students are engaged in fascinating arenas of work and, as they hear each other articulate what they are doing in their individual spaces, it is evident that, as a community of scholars, they have the potential to carve out innovative and distinctive pathways that could be transformative for African descendants in education and the wider community.

What has also been clearly evident to Dr Beckles-Raymond and me in coordinating this network over the last few years is that far too many British academic institutions are institutionally ignorant and negligent in how they treat their Black postgraduate students. We operate our group utilising Chatham House rules to enable students to speak freely and to share ideas and feelings without fear. Far too often the group has to offer students practical support and nurture concerning how to deal with isolation, racism, lack of understanding of the students work and an overburdening of Black students with additional work burdens without the concrete offers of postdoctoral positions or other jobs afterwards. We step in as much as we can, advising students, reading their work, undertaking mock vivas and providing emotional and academic support, all outside our regular day jobs – the usual story of Black workers doing extra labour to counter the deficits of institutionally racist systems.

Ironically, given all the work that we have undertaken in this area primarily as volunteers and latterly with the support of Leading Routes, when UK Research and Innovation (UKRI) and the Office for Students decided that they would address inequalities in support for Black doctoral students, our associated networks were bypassed. I could be bitter and, in a sense, I am frustrated by the performative tunes that institutions play in response to racial inequity and injustice. However, in the network I have seen students we have supported graduate, get jobs, write books and advance the cause of our communities, and that fills me with an overwhelming sense of gratitude and fulfilment to all those that have been a part of this journey.

In running the ADPN I have seen Black students thrive and become re-energised and purposed because they have been in a space that loves them as people, admires and respects their work as scholars and understands that their Black genius is nourished by being in community. Higher education institutions are failing Black students because they fail to acknowledge that their spaces are alienating and isolating for students whose cultural identities are often at the core of what motivates them to undertake the studies that they do. ADPN and sister networks, such as the one run by Dr Maria Althea Rivas at the School of Oriental and African Studies, are bringing students through in spite of, not because of. We operate in and outside of the system, because we want students to succeed and advance knowledge to improve the lived experience of our communities, but we also recognise that they need private spaces to breathe, decompress and vent about the toxicity that they have been exposed to in White institutional academic spaces.

We long for the day when we can have fully Black majority-led departments, Black research centres and African Diaspora Postgraduate Networks across all regions of the UK. But until then we will continue to recognise Black genius, listen to Black voices and nurture Black visions from within our African diasporic space.

Reflections on Part III and prompts for action

Jacqueline Darkwa

The journey of a doctoral degree is no mean feat. Those inclined to embark on this journey do so at the risk of discrimination amid isolation and loneliness. As you have read in the essays in this part, the void created by higher education institutions is filled by Black-led academic support groups and networks. They do this in addition to undertaking the highest academic challenge of their careers, with minimal support from the institutions themselves. If this work was to be appropriately supported and integrated into institutional practice, what would that mean for Black and other marginalised academics?

Each of the essay writers had to find their own support networks, or go out and entirely create what did not already exist; the energy exerted in this effort should not be overlooked. It is long and hard labour to develop and maintain a safe space for Black academics across different disciplines and journeys – if this effort was liberated, where else could Black academics be sharing their excellence?

PART IV

Academic support: the right thing, in the right place, at the right time

De-Shaine Murray

The following set of chapters detail the powerful role that individuals and support systems within academia have played in the successful development and progression of Black PhD students. Having appropriate support while progressing through the various stages of academia is vital for the development of all scholars, as many rules and practices in these spaces are often unwritten, complex and require extensive training to traverse. Whether it be a supervisor, programme or the work of a department, positive guidance helps to ensure the success of all students. These support systems are even more critical for Black students who often navigate environments where they are in the minority. Their minoritisation can develop into a consuming feeling that wears them down, affecting their wellbeing and continuation through the academic pipeline. The correct support can therefore help counteract this isolation and marginalisation, which is all too common a feature of academic spaces in the UK.

Suitable academic support can take many forms but amounts to the same end product – the increased retention of students, who feel empowered, confident and are able to progress further. At the beginning of this part, Simone's chapter demonstrates the power of effective outreach, where an institution made a concerted effort to interface with underserved schools within London. This, in addition to the support she subsequently received from her academic mentor and her PhD supervisor after being diagnosed with rheumatoid arthritis, were critical for her continuation within academic research. Next, Angela gives her account of being uplifted after being worn down from a previous academic experience, and the deliberate decision she made to choose a supportive environment. This choice, often a strong consideration for many prospective Black students was vindicated by the confidence her supervisors instilled in her. In Peggy's chapter we see the assistance and support of multiple supervisors that allows for her creative research choices, which went against the status quo, to come to fruition. Her work has gone on to be screened publicly and celebrated nationally. Conversely, Rees' account shows the importance of vital interventions by academics and a department when conflicts arise during supervision and the transformative effect that being proactive can have on a scholar's wellbeing and growth. This part then concludes with Clíona, whose chapter celebrates her supervisor's support and belief in her that enabled her progression to the PhD level, despite various obstacles and challenges.

Equipping Black academics with the right tools is essential to them realising long and fruitful careers within academia, if they so choose. Effective academic support is therefore crucial for the retention of Black PhD scholars and must be replicated and expanded where possible. The experiences and, by extension, lives of many Black PhD students would be changed for the better if this was made a reality. In this part, we see examples of the right support, in the right place, and at the right time.

19

Reaching beyond the horizon: being inspired to succeed against the odds

Simone Webb

I was first introduced to higher education through the University College London Horizons programme, an outreach programme for underserved schools in London. Inspired by meeting Black students at Horizons, I applied for and eventually completed my Master in Science (MSci) in Biological Sciences. This experience is testament to how important the visibility of Black people in academic spaces has been to me since the beginning of my journey. I was diagnosed with rheumatoid arthritis during my master's and I am now completing a PhD. Being transparent and setting expectations has been paramount for my progress in academia as a Black disabled woman. I would not have been able to choose this path for myself without having strong support systems, which reinforced my sense of belonging when my educational institutions could not or would not.

My personal inspiration to succeed

I am a proud descendent of the Windrush generation, who uprooted their lives to provide opportunities for their children as economic migrants from Jamaica to the UK.

My paternal grandmother, Viola Webb (née Lawrence), was raised in Nine Mile in the heart of St Ann, Jamaica, where the soil is red and rich in bauxite. Viola settled a few miles west in Alva, where she worked as a homemaker and had 12 children, including my father, Lincoln. In my father's early 20s, he worked in electrical engineering, before transitioning into security work in the Jamaican capital, Kingston.

My maternal grandmother, Gloria Lee (née Meghoo), was raised in Kingston, but worked abroad as a typist in the USA and the UK for much of her adult life. Gloria first came to the UK as part of the Windrush generation in 1960, but her children, including my mother, Jennifer, were raised in Kingston. In my mother's early 20s, she's grew an affection for a security guard called Lincoln, whom she'd met on one of her regular solo trips to the local football stadium. They married in 1989 and moved to London with a small toddler in tow.

I was born in the 1990s, Lincoln and Jennifer's fourth child, and raised with my four siblings in council housing in Lambeth, south London. During my childhood, Lambeth had a large Black population, comprising 26 per cent of the borough's total, so I had a more diverse impression of the UK's ethnic demographics than would have been the case across London, which had a 13 per cent Black population, or the UK, which had a 3 per cent Black population (2011 UK Census). I was an energetic teenager and had a variety of interests. My head was buried in books, but I also busily tried my hand at dressmaking, piloting in the air cadets, singing in community theatre productions, and youth advocacy in charities.

I thrived in school, where I completed my GCSEs at the top of my year and made long-term close friends. I was interested in the idea of university; however, there was little awareness or promotion of non-vocational degree options in my school. The understanding was that those with hopes to attend university who excelled in science would apply for medicine and that the linguists would apply for law. As such, my main aim at this time was to become a medic, since I favoured the sciences over the humanities. This career plan was precariously grounded, as many of my friends and I were the first in our families to attend university and received free school meals; our professional career decisions often amounted to theory and guesswork.

I was formally introduced to higher education through a pilot university outreach programme for underserved schools in London. This is where I learnt about the spectrum of non-medical paths into STEM careers for the first time. I was in awe of the Black undergraduate and postgraduate students I met – they seemed like mythical beings to me. These encounters with Black university students enabled me to see myself in their position, and to reflect on my own future career motivations and ambitions. I was eventually inspired to take a leap of faith and abandon the vague promise of medicine as my sole career option. I decided that I would apply to study for a degree in Biology.

With a new academic plan, I gained entrance to a partially selective state sixth form in Wandsworth borough. It became painfully clear that I had massive gaps in academic knowledge, which was unknown territory for me. At this time, I was also getting to grips with being one of few Black people in the room; an experience that, prior to this, I had only confronted for days at a time. Divisions across socio-economic lines also became clearer to me at sixth form, where I had my first introduction to students with means, access, and a startlingly easy understanding of places like Oxbridge through close personal links. My sixth form experience meant that I increasingly saw myself as an unlikely candidate for UK higher education. It was sustained participation in outreach programmes that was important for me. Here I was continually challenged to see the ways in which higher education could be a positive benefit and that I could develop in that environment. The visibility of Black people in UK academic spaces has been transformative for me since the beginning of my journey. Encouragement from outreach programmes went a long way toward my decision to eventually study Biological Sciences at university. My university was a predominantly White space; I was one of two Black people on my course (both of us women) and was never taught by a Black lecturer or professor. I became increasingly familiar with this isolation throughout my studies, though I still found it difficult.

It is with some concern that I look back and realise how quickly familiarity can turn into perceived normalcy. How much more disruptive could the transition into a White university space have been for me had I not moved to a different sixth form? During my undergraduate degree, I was hyper-aware of my presence in the institution as a recipient of targeted outreach work. Out of duty to the incoming students that were in the position I had been in,

I interviewed for and successfully became a student ambassador in the first month of my enrolment. It was satisfying work to come full circle as the 'mythical being' for those students, just as previous student ambassadors had been for me.

Nevertheless, the longer I stayed in the academic space, the more disillusioned I became. During my undergraduate studies, my university was investigated for hosting a eugenics conference with White supremacist speakers; events such as this undid a lot of the trust that I had in universities and outreach programmes. I worried at times that I was encouraging the students to enter spaces that were not wholly welcoming to them. I took care to be honest with my experience as much as possible, while not deterring them from opportunities that would be beneficial for their scientific education. This tightrope was a difficult one to walk. I am sure I got it wrong multiple times.

In the fourth year of my degree, I was diagnosed with rheumatoid arthritis, which was a massive upheaval to my identity and lifestyle. My 'new normal' meant I had to learn how to manage long-term pain, attend clinics on a weekly basis for testing and appointments, and trial dozens of medications including self-administered injections – which often failed. I leant heavily on my partner, friends and family for support while adapting to this new part-time job of managing chronic illness. On a practical level, my chronic pain was exacerbated by London crowds and inaccessible transport services; taking the tube or bus to lectures was becoming increasingly difficult. Following advice from my academic mentor, I got in touch with student services, who encouraged me to apply for a disabled student's allowance with Student Finance England (SFE). SFE provided critical support for me, including a taxi support service, a home desk with ergonomic set-up and accessible software in order to dictate my dissertation on days that I could not type. Personal support systems alongside concrete interventions from SFE ultimately prevented me from quitting my course.

Following this tumultuous year, I graduated with first-class honours and restructured priorities. I decided to apply for funded PhD programmes and to disclose my illness upon interview. I am the first to study for a postgraduate degree in my immediate family, so I approached the PhD application process in a way similar to my undergraduate application: fairly naïve to the realities but equipped with a list of questions. I was accepted onto a Bioinformatics and Immunology PhD programme, for which I moved across the country to begin in 2018. My primary supervisor is a woman of colour who was open to me working from home, if needed, as soon as I raised this as a requirement at interview. My PhD research is now part of a global consortium effort, where I use coding to understand how we form our immune systems during prenatal development.

Being transparent and setting expectations has been paramount for my progress in academia as a disabled Black woman. I am acutely aware I would not have had the freedom to choose an academic path without participating in university-led outreach programmes promoting the visibility of Black people in UK academic spaces. Academia would not have been feasible for me without study adaptations supported by SFE and my supervision team. Access to strong support systems reinforced my sense of belonging when educational institutions could not or would not.

20

In and out of prison: my personal research journey of being a Black woman, researching Black women

Angela Charles

This essay looks at my PhD journey undertaking research on Black women's experiences in prison. Firstly, I will discuss the decision to apply to study at the Open University, explaining the conscious decision to choose the Open University after studying at the University of Oxford for my master's. The essay will discuss my supervisors as my main support mechanism; from building up my confidence as an academic to applying for access to the female prison estate. The final part of the essay will look at the struggles I have encountered, including negotiating prison fieldwork while pregnant, as well as reflecting on my positionality as a Black woman researching Black women in prison.

My journey is incomplete, but the support and challenges I have experienced thus far, combined with the important stories of the women interviewed, act as a driving force to ensure my PhD reaches completion and is heard.

My personal journey

Luck, determination, intelligence, motivation, strength, resilience, courage: these are the words that come to mind when I think about how I got to where I am today. I have earned my place as an academic, yet it is still something I have to negotiate and prove to both myself and the field I strive to be a part of.

My PhD journey has been one with challenges along the way, but I have received great support – from the application process right through to where I am today. The application process is a good place to start as it highlights the encouragement I received, and the ways in which two lecturers went above and beyond their role. Having nearly finished my master's degree at a top-rated university, I was feeling rather low in confidence about my place in academia, when in fact it should have been the opposite. Completing my master's at this university had shaken my belief in my academic ability; I did not feel a sense of belonging within academia. Additionally, I did not feel good enough to be in the same field as those who had taught me. I felt my work was below par and that it required a lot more developing if I wanted to succeed in academia. It is down to interpretation as to whether it was my own lack of self-confidence that was to blame, or partly the fault of the institution for not recognising their processes had damaged my own sense of self-worth.

Seeing the part-time studentship offered at the Open University was a blessing and a curse. It seemed like such a good opportunity to conduct research and write my thesis on Black women in prison, something I had wanted to do at the master's level, but had been unable to in the ten-month timeframe. Wanting some reassurance before committing to applying, I sent an email to one of the lecturers who had put their email address as a point of contact for advice. Having not heard back, I took this as a sign to not apply and took it no further. It was not until a few weeks before the deadline when I received an email from the lecturer encouraging me to apply. He was showing interest in my research idea, and even offered to look over my application. He had even contacted another lecturer at the same department to also provide assistance. It was the reassurance I had been looking for, and so I decided to apply. Receiving that advice and encouragement may have not been much for those two academics, but to a Black female academic in the early stages of her journey it was invaluable.

The application looked daunting. I needed to have an idea of the methodology, research aims, hypotheses and so on. There were times I questioned whether I was 'academic enough' and whether to continue with my application. I sent my application to the lecturers, awaiting rejection through the lens of constructive feedback. I was surprised to receive positive and encouraging feedback, with realistic changes to better align my application with the criteria the university was looking for. This was the first turning point in my journey. The time they had invested in me, the support provided, and the insider knowledge was invaluable. I do not doubt that the aforementioned gave me that fighting chance to be successful in my application.

Fast forward a few years into my part-time PhD and my experience of the application process to gain access to the prisons. I had been warned that it was a long and difficult process, and I did not think I would be one of the lucky ones who would be granted access. It was another thorough and lengthy application where I felt I was having to prove my academic worth and my knowledge. This time round I had the support of two different lecturers, my supervisors. They talked me through the process step by step, imparting their own knowledge of these types of applications and giving me examples to go by. My supervisors looked at my draft application and together amended and went through it with precision and scrutiny.

Most importantly, my supervisors provided the assurance that I needed to complete the application. Their kind words of encouragement, regular check-ins, constructive feedback on my work and their knowledge all spurred me on to persevere. I received push back from the prison, but my supervisors were there straight away, providing guidance on what tweaks to make and what concessions to accept. It was a proud moment when it was confirmed I had been granted access and would be able to conduct my research the way I wanted. More importantly, it was a proud moment when it sunk in that I would be able to interview Black female prisoners whose stories I so desperately wanted to hear. It felt like I had reached a massive turning point in my research journey. I had successfully overcome a huge obstacle; now my research goal was becoming a reality.

I received further support when I faced another obstacle during my research. I had to navigate my prison fieldwork and PhD study while pregnant and partly on maternity leave. My supervisors were encouraging, supportive and adaptive. Whenever I stressed my urgency to do something during this period my supervisors matched my pace and my urgency. This helped me to realise it was possible to still make progress during this period. They accommodated me on my maternity leave and my son attended supervisions with me on their request. Additionally, when something had to be delayed, my supervisors were reassuring in advising me that I was still on track and achieving my goals. They were always on hand to remind me how much I had managed to achieve despite the setbacks, challenges and constant juggling of my commitments. Once again, that sense of worthiness that I needed when I was having my moments of doubt was present, and reinforced my duty to continue my research in this important area.

It has been invaluable to have supervisors who are genuinely passionate about my research and research topic. I have never once felt that I had to explain the importance of my research. Discussions with my supervisors have always been insightful and in depth; there is not an area of discourse that was shied away from, which was so important for my research.

There are a lot of things from my experience that can be applied to prospective Black research candidates and Black individuals currently embarking on a PhD across all academic institutions. The first thing is about worth. From the beginning of the application process, I was made to feel like I was a worthy candidate for a PhD, and to feel like I was worthy to be in academia. Lastly, I was made to feel like my research was worthy and significant. I think this worthiness is vital as Black researchers navigate a field where they are a minority, where they feel uncertain, and where they have something to prove.

When conducting research, support from supervisors is vital, especially if the individual is new to the world of fieldwork. Reassurance is key during this period to ensure the student is supported and that they do not withdraw from their research or academia.

One final point worth noting is that Black research students need to feel like they are more than just a number and a statistic. We do not want to be that Black, Asian and ethnic minoritised (BAME) individual conducting a PhD and feel that we have been selected because we are underrepresented; we want to feel that we have been chosen on merit, because of our intellect, our drive and our novel research proposals. We have so much to offer in the academic field. My story is one where I have been fortunate to have supervisors who have created and facilitated an environment where I can flourish and reach my potential.

21

Not in this alone: being supported to break down barriers to PhD success

Peggy Warren

My PhD examined Black British and Black Caribbean women's experiences of National Health Service (NHS) work-based education and its impact on their professional identities. I had two White female supervisors; they were very supportive of my intention to break from the conventions of what a PhD thesis should look like when using performative autoethnography to present the women as characters in fictional settings. A non-conventional approach was important for me as it meant that my 'academic' work would be accessible to both academics and non-academics, as well as contribute to the discourses on systemic inequities. Since completion in 2017, a scene of the autoethnography has been screened at the Birmingham Repertory Theatre; another scene has been produced as a podcast, which has been used on radio and in presentations nationally for International Women's Day 2020.

I would like to share with prospective students lessons on making academic work accessible to non-academic research participants and our wider communities.

I was born in Birmingham in the UK in the 1960s. My father, who had left school aged 11 following the death of his father in the 1940s, has a brilliant mind and guided me into education as a profession. After my O-levels, I pursued a further education teacher's certificate course, followed by a range of subject specialist stand-alone higher education modules. I studied part time for over a decade completing my Bachelor of Arts (BA) Honours and Master of Arts (MA). One professor who marked my MA dissertation ended her assessment with the following: 'Must publish. Consider pursuing a PhD.'

I did not know what a PhD was. Following exploration, I was amused that she would make such a suggestion. That was certainly not part of my plan. I felt that the personal and institutional barriers to me undertaking a PhD would be: (1) finances and support; (2) my dislike of PhD theses as dense volumes of work inaccessible to non-academics.

I have worked in the NHS for over 20 years, facilitating a range of education programmes from English for Speakers of Other Languages to Leadership and Management. Throughout my MA and PhD studies I worked in an NHS trust in the Midlands as the only Black tutor in the Learning and Development department. A number of my students had progressed from my work-based programme to a higher education part-time, two-year, funded foundation degree on day release. This widening participation initiative was designed to upskill NHS staff and address work shortages in the field of nursing. The promise was that, on completion, those in the first two cohorts would be appointed to new, higher paid roles. After a number of intakes, I noticed a pattern of withdrawals at year one, predominantly among Black women. As a practitioner researcher, I wanted to explore and share the women's experiences. So, I met with my MA professor and one of her colleagues to pitch my idea for a research project. And so my PhD journey began.

At the beginning of my doctoral studies, I questioned whether I had contributed to setting the women up to fail. I carried a sense of responsibility for them. I felt that, as their tutor, our stories were entwined: we were all the first in our families to attend university; we had long histories of working in the NHS; and we were students at the same Midlands university. I was a self-funded, part-time, postgraduate student working compressed hours, so I had a day dedicated to my studies.

During my research, it transpired that the failure to complete the programme was not about the women's abilities. The widening participation initiative had failed to deliver on its promise to place the first two cohorts of graduates in new professional higher salaried positions. As a result, the Black women became disillusioned; they feared that when they completed the course, their labour would be exploited. I knew that I wanted to present the stories in a format that made them accessible to the women informing the study and ordinary members of the wider communities from which we originated. I also wanted my work to contribute to activism. These commitments were non-negotiable even though neither I, nor my supervisors knew how I could do what I wanted to do.

My supervisors were White women, and one was American with a history of involvement in racial justice movements. I organised and attended all my monthly supervisions; the supervisors' approaches to support were very different but in an extremely helpful way. One was my challenger as I formulated and presented my ideas; the other was my detail-obsessed guide. One of them introduced me to the works of Professors Carolyn Ellis and Arthur Bochner, who were among the academics working to change paradigms in social science research. Through Ellis' work, *The ethnographic I*, I found autoethnography. Autoethnography is 'research, writing, story and method that connect the autobiographical and personal to the cultural, social and political' (Ellis, 2004). After I contacted Professor Ellis, she invited me to the International Congress of Qualitative Inquiry (ICQI) annual conference. My supervisor supported my funding application to attend the conference in Chicago, Illinois – first in 2014 to explore autoethnographic writing then, in 2016, as a contributor. The conference gave me access to a supportive and international research community.

Being part-time, I worked in isolation a lot, and that was one of my biggest challenges. I used my non-working day to access the full-time PhD students' office on campus and, though I did not belong, I gained great insights. My decision to use Black feminism as my methodological stance and autoethnography in the form of ethnodrama as the mechanism[1] for presenting my data did not faze my supervisors at all. I felt that it enriched my PhD experience, as my supervisors and I were learning together. We were all on a journey on a road less travelled. My supervisors were great at providing feedback on my work. We did not always agree; but when we did not agree, I owned my decisions.

Striving to write unconventionally was scary and messy, but I did not want to invest my life researching and producing knowledge that would only be read by academics. I felt strongly that I had to carve out my way of reinventing how our stories were presented. I wanted my work to be rigorous and academically credible and, at the same time, I wanted it to reflect where parts of my culture were being subverted in places like academia: our oral history, for example. My thesis was interrupted with what I described as 'irruptions' (Koro-Ljungberg, 2016) – occasions when I either incorporated my feelings or some wisdom that was prevalent in our communities and generally passed on through oral traditions.

In my final year, one of my supervisors became very unwell, but she still attended most of my supervisions remotely and provided guidance. In that year, I shared my research at several conferences. The discussions that followed each presentation boosted my confidence and helped me sharpen the way I spoke about my study. Approximately two months before my viva voce, a postdoctoral researcher read my thesis and engaged me in conversation around my approaches and choices. The woman was of Chinese heritage and felt that autoethnography would be an ideal research methodology to write and present the intergenerational voices of her cultural community. This was a reciprocally useful exercise as I had the opportunity to really make my message on my methodological choices clear. Prior to my viva, my supervisor organised a 'dummy run' with faculty members. In the dummy viva they focused on my methodology and data presentation. I had expected my real viva to be challenging because I had broken conventions. It was challenging, but I actually enjoyed it. I passed with minor corrections, which I completed in three months.

To remain true about my work contributing to social activism, I ended my thesis explicitly arguing that the work had not been completed; the end of the thesis was merely the end of the academic process. It was important to state that the work would continue through a range of interactions and coalitions. After graduation, one of my supervisors introduced me to a contact at a local theatre company. She then introduced me to a young Black producer, Daniel Bailey, at the Birmingham Repertory Theatre. As part of a broader initiative showcasing the works of new writers, Daniel supported me in the reworking of a scene of my ethnodrama, which was performed on stage with professional actresses. The research participants and members of our wider Black community attended the performance. Within a year of completing my studies, the ethnodrama was published as a book and the women have been retelling their own stories in public meetings, including at an NHS International Women's Day event in London 2020.

I am proud of my commitment to autoethnographic writing. My work showed those coming after me what was possible. In the summer of 2020, two years after my graduation, I was contacted by a young Black woman studying for an MPhil in Education at the University of Cambridge. We had a number of conversations about my work and her aspirations. In her 2020 MPhil dissertation acknowledgement she wrote: 'Thank you, God, for Dr Peggy Warren. The mentor that blessed me with attentive ears and wise words. Her boldness, her example, her advice, that dared me to do it differently.'

Now my mentee is embarking on her own PhD journey. My PhD journey was an incredibly positive one. My interest in the women who contributed and being a self-funded student meant I was really focused and disciplined. My supervisors, participants and ICQI colleagues and family formed a great support base for my eventual success.

Note
[1] An ethnodrama is the written transformation and adaptation of ethnographic research data into a dramatic playscript staged as a live, public theatrical performance.

References
Ellis, C. (2004). *The ethnographic I. A methodological novel about autoethnography*. New York: Altamira Press.

Koro-Ljungberg, M. (2016). *Reconceptualizing qualitative research: methodologies without methodology*. Los Angeles: Sage.

22

When seasons change: dealing with a change in my situation while studying for a PhD

Rees Johnson

My first supervisory team was made up of two academics, both seemingly 'expert' in assisted death. However, my thesis was not just about assisted death – assisted death was merely the Trojan horse. In fact, my PhD could have used any other of the top ten bioethical issues; however, it was the core of my thesis that most interested me. I had opted to utilise the work of Michel Foucault to look at assisted death in a new way. To break what I perceived to be a rhetorical circularity that had resulted in superficial gestures of progress rather than significant shifts in thinking. I did not think that what I was doing, importing the work of Foucault. was actually that radical. For anyone who is interested in power or the intersection of political theory and the body, Foucault seems an obvious choice. Unless, of course, you have never actually studied him.

My first year looking back was pretty traumatic – the intellectual violence that I was subjected to had a serious and profound effect on me. I was tasked, in the first six months of my PhD, with having to justify the value of Michel Foucault to someone who had never read him; and to apologise for Michel Foucault to someone who regarded him as an obscurantist and who had never, it came to be understood, had a tangential understanding of his oeuvre. The feedback I got on my work was harsh, overly critical, unsupportive and demoralising. When I compared my work to my colleagues, no one could actually see any difference in the quality – it was just as good or just as poor as everyone else's and yet, for some reason, I felt singled out. It did not matter how many times I rewrote my papers or pivoted, it was never enough. By the end of my first year, I had a word bank of almost 100,000 – which was about 90,000 more words than my colleagues in the first year had written. It felt like no one wanted to see me thrive. My two supervisors had made their minds up about me and about my PhD. Eventually, however, I got a third supervisor who came on board who had a much broader understanding of my theoretical framework. They understood the value of my approach, of applying a Foucauldian lens to the study of assisted death. The problem we had was that my main supervisor had deferred to the second on the basis they knew what they were talking about; and so it became a battle between me and my newly appointed third supervisor, and my primary supervisor and secondary supervisor.

While all this was taking place, I was undergoing something physiologically and psychologically, which I could not explain at first. It started with feeling spaced out and exhausted. Then I started experiencing hot flushes that washed over my entire body. Eventually, this led to sustained periods of disassociation. I was losing my mind, and it was a slow progressive loss. This meant I was not able to draw connections between my triggers and my panic attacks. The fabric of my mind, under the immense pressure and scrutiny, was fraying; I did not know that what I was experiencing was connected to that pressure. For months it felt like I was on the verge of a stroke; the only way to stop myself from having the stroke was to contain the panic and try not to give into it. I would have panic attacks in the supermarket, on the walk to my building, or in the common room. While all this was happening, I was trying to do my very best to make it seem like I was not falling apart. I tried to rationalise the experience as something other than what it was. I had never had a panic attack before and what little I knew of them was not reflected in what I was experiencing. Nine months into my PhD, I finally drew the connection between my trigger and my panic attacks: it was my supervisors. The thought of having to send work to them, speak to them, think about what they had said and what they might say, filled me with dread. On one occasion I submitted some work to my first and third supervisor and asked if they would look at it before I sent it to my second supervisor, who was the most critical. My first supervisor responded to my request by forwarding my work and the email I had sent to the second supervisor. My second supervisor replied criticising my attempt to undermine them, when in truth I was trying to preserve my sanity. Finally, my third supervisor had reached their limit and questioned the second supervisor as to why they felt the need to be so critical and unhelpful, to which the second supervisor responded: 'I'm trying to be helpful because I see a lot of myself in Rees.' This was the justification for the intellectual trauma and violence: it was being done for my own good.

Much of my childhood was miserable and, for many years, I was made to feel worthless. To escape this misery, I spent a lot of time at the library – reading everything and anything I could. I fortified my mind and made myself impenetrable. My intellect and thirst for knowledge somehow acted as a buffer and created a symbolic space for me to seek refuge in, a place where I knew those who sought to cause me harm could not reach. Why my first year of the PhD did what it did to me, and how my two supervisors were able to cause significant harm to me, is because they were both able to reach into that symbolic space and inflict the harm that my abusers could not. So those feelings of neglect and intellectual bullying were suddenly at once able to penetrate the walls I had spent my childhood building and my teenage years defending. Eventually my first supervisor ignored my emails, pretended not to see me in the corridors. And so, in a way, what they did to me in that first year was far more significant and serious than what had happened to me growing up, and made worse because I just did not see it coming.

Prior to my upgrade in June, I had a meeting with my supervisory team, as all students do prior to their annual review. I left that meeting thinking everything was going to be fine and that we were all on the same page. My submission was almost of doctoral standard – not perfect, but enough to get into the second year. Little did I know that between that meeting and my annual review my two supervisors had changed their mind and failed to notify me. I went into my annual review excited that I had done enough to pass. But when I got into the meeting, the mood was very sombre. My first and second supervisor informed me that I would be downgraded to an MPhil. In this meeting I would discover my supervisor's justification for the first time. I was made to read my supervisor's comments in front of my review panel. My annual review panel was conflicted: once again it was my third supervisor and me versus my first and second supervisor. Consequently, at my third supervisor's insistence, my work was reviewed by an external reviewer, who recommended that I be progressed into the second year.

Where am I now? I am in my third and final year with a winning project and a winning supervisory team. My third supervisor became my first supervisor and the department drafted in a critical legal scholar to be my second. I have two new supervisors now, neither of whom are experts in assisted death, but are experts in my theoretical framework. As well as supervising my project, they also have had the added task of walking back the damage that was done to me – a job that neither of them should have had to do. Notwithstanding this, however, I am grateful that, when it mattered the most, my department and my school sprang into action to correct the mistake that had been made. While I am yet to receive an apology from my first and second supervisor, this experience has taught me a lot: sometimes when White scholarship is confronted with Black scholarship it does not understand; it will go to extreme lengths to destabilise and delegitimise – even at the risk of seeming unqualified.

23

Believing that the impossible is possible: my story of being supported to succeed

Clíona Kelly

My journey through education did not originally focus on the traditional sciences in school. It was the support of others, as well as the opportunities and experiences that changed this for me and led me to the field I am now in. At A-level I studied Media, Performing Arts and Psychology. My undergraduate was in Psychology and I failed a final-year module called 'Brain Imaging'. On paper, I am not the typical student to go on to do a PhD. My post-graduation plans were changed as a lecturer was impressed and convinced me to stay to do a master's in Cognitive Neuroscience. This provided me with the tools to apply for a PhD, where I was offered two studentships. Having someone see the bigger picture and believe in you is so powerful for self-belief and ambition. Taking these opportunities and working through these educational spaces, you witness the lack of representation as a whole. Being privileged in that position can weigh heavily on an individual for a range of reasons, and preparing to deal with those can be tough.

In today's society it is often assumed that you will attend university after finishing your mandatory education. Most prospective students are encouraged to choose a broad subject and not to constrain their future prospects by studying something that is too specific. And so some students do just that: they attend, get their degree and explore the working world with their qualifications. I was a little different. At the time when

I undertook my undergraduate studies, I wanted to become a child psychologist and I knew that I needed to earn the 'Dr' title in order to do so. What I did not understand was the path to get there. This prompted me to apply for a placement year (an excellent decision that was largely pushed by the university), where I would gain experience working as an honorary clinical psychologist for the National Health Service. I did not enjoy this role and quickly realised my image of what I thought a psychologist was was incorrect. When I returned to my final year of study, I was unsure how to move forward. I knew I wanted to be abroad, and so I applied for a government teaching role in Hong Kong and was ready to station my life in Asia while occasionally travelling around in my spare time. The dream was to be in a hot country, working with children, and travelling to incredible places on my holidays. What would my career look like? I was not sure. Did I actually want to become a teacher? Again, not sure.

Everything took a spin during one of my final lectures. I had received an email from the professor of a joint attention module who was impressed with my questions during the class. In his email he offered me supervision on the Cognitive Neuroscience master's programme. For months I was riddled with nerves and apprehension around my skills and ability to complete this qualification. I went back and forth with friends and family to double check whether this was the right avenue for me and finally came to my decision to go ahead and enrol.

Then I received my final year results.

I had failed a module called 'Brain Imaging'. I thought 'Who would want to supervise a student that failed the very module they were going on to study at postgraduate level?' Of course, imposter syndrome kicked in and I immediately sent an email to the professor explaining the situation, and that I would understand if he no longer wanted to supervise me. Instead of being dismissive, he organised a meeting and we went over the mistake I had made. I was then reassured that this did not matter. We would be continuing with the master's, with a brain imaging technique in combination with virtual reality, equipment I had not used before and did not have a technical background in. Over the summer, I began learning about virtual reality in an attempt to learn the foundations I needed to complete this experiment.

Technology, coding and using virtual reality were completely new to me. But in the grand scheme of studying for a master's, this did not matter. We all had the same amount of time to develop and create our projects, irrespective of past education, skills and knowledge. However, I also had the financial aspect to take into consideration. This is not uncommon for Black students and is often a barrier in completing higher education. I was very lucky; the new government postgraduate loan had just been released and so I was able to cover my tuition fees with that.

However, I still needed to afford to live and so I went searching for a part-time job that paid enough while studying for a full-time master's. I was eventually offered a graduate role within the university that focused on outreach in schools and colleges. For me, this was perfect because they were completely aware that I was studying and I could be completely transparent with my situation. It also tapped into my passion for working with younger students and encouraging them into higher education. On paper the situation seemed perfect; I was grateful for the opportunity from my supervisor but also from a financial aspect.

In fact, this was one of the most stressful and isolating times I have ever experienced. Balancing working and studying is difficult enough, but when that work is outreach, it has an additional level of responsibility, particularly when you are passionate and emotionally invested. Through my time studying in higher and further education, I have witnessed the stark decrease of Black students and lower socio-economic status students, as you climb the academic ladder. Of course, there are several reasons for this, but a recurring theme is the lack of support from within the academy. Thankfully, I gained two close friends from my graduate role who helped me through the year, by reminding me of why I was doing it and the importance of moving forward. This was accompanied by a strong support system consisting of my friends and family in my hometown of Bristol. These factors, alongside the unquestioned support of a supervisor who could see my potential and the bigger picture, steered me to my PhD.

Reflecting on my experience completing the master's, I overall had enjoyed the project aspect of the curriculum. For me, this was what was important in carrying on to the PhD level. After finishing the master's and coming back from travelling, I began searching for studentships and was offered two places. One was in a centre for doctoral training. Days after, I was offered funding with my supervisor, co-funded by the Engineering and Physical Sciences Research Council. Both PhDs were based around the intersection of computer science and neuroscience, combining virtual reality and electroencephalography to investigate social cognition. One thing that has stuck with me was the fact that both were combined with computer science. This is a subject that I had no formal background in and so it was quite the realisation to me that it was an area that I could go into.

Making the decision on which PhD to go with was initially difficult. I was conflicted as to whether I should stay with what I knew or go and experience another university and supervisor – especially as I had done my undergraduate and master's in the same place. But I had witnessed the impact of poor supervision on others' PhD topics, the individuals themselves and the overall experience. This is even more prevalent for Black students and is a common narrative in many of the accounts I had heard. As a result, my choice of supervisor was the deciding factor. Upon reflection, the energy and belief that came from my master's supervisor was really a driving force in my academic aspirations and, given that, I decided to stay where I was.

Since then, it has become even more apparent to me how salient the role of a supervisor is. Not only in the completion of your PhD and to drive your work ethic, but in the goals you set for yourself and what you believe to be achievable. Before completing the master's and applying for PhDs, I did not understand what a PhD *really* was and how competitive it was for funding. As a result, I did not realise the level of skill that was required to complete a PhD, let alone to compete for funding with a competitive CV. With the encouragement of my supervisor, I was able to build a competitive CV for the academic market. This experience highlighted how naïve my understanding of the process was; going through that process alone, without someone who understood the academic world, would have been near enough impossible.

Having a good supervisor is not just about the simple things, that is getting along and being friends. It is also about having someone who can manage your expectations, see the bigger picture and push you towards it, even when you cannot see it. This has been even more evident while studying through a global pandemic. During intense times like these, you can observe how senior members of staff react to the situation and this is telling of their true beliefs. I strongly encourage prospective students, particularly those of a Black background, to research their supervisors and build a support network both inside and outside academia. This can be done by getting involved in online campaigns such as the #BlackInX weeks, but also joining collectives like African-Caribbean Research Collective (@ACRC_UK) and the PhD Hive (@ThePhDHive).

Reflections on Part IV and prompts for action

De-Shaine Murray

> Why is this support not common? It is a damning indictment of our system that such positive stories from Black PhD students are the exception and not the rule. Why are best practices not being adopted sector wide? Introductory programmes such as Horizons, outlined in Simone's chapter, can inspire further study and should be replicated across the country. Once enrolled, the behaviour of supervisors can be the sole difference between failure for a student and success. Supervisors therefore need to be adequately trained. Rees' chapter shows how mismanagement can have stark consequences for a trainee's mental and physical health and how the same person under the correct guidance can flourish and excel. The toxicity, which seems to be so prevalent in our sector, needs to be rooted out and replaced with the proactiveness and holistic support detailed in this part. Why is this not a feature of our system?

PART V

Reflections at the completion of the PhD journey

Madina Wane

In the last four parts, we have seen the varied stories of Black scholars prior to and upon entering the academy. The chapters in this part are reflective accounts from researchers who have embarked on the PhD journey and arrived at the other end. Each contributor explores their trials, tribulations and celebrations of completing a PhD, and what the future holds for Black scholars beyond the PhD.

The stories of the Black PhD scholars are much larger than individual successes and challenges – they are shaped by the families and communities that came before them. Though Black scholars come from many different backgrounds, all share ancestral journeys impacted by a painful combination of slavery, colonialism and state violence. In spite, and indeed as a result, of this, Black heritage also involves resistance to these oppressions. Within Black British communities, there is a rich history, and ongoing resistance to oppression through creation of community-led education projects. Starting from the 1960s, members of the African-Caribbean community set up their own independent after-school programmes to support the learning of Black students, but also to centre Black culture, history and politics in their education. This movement, known as the Black Supplementary School programme, was a response to the inadequacies of the UK state education system in supporting Black students (Coard, 1971; Andrews, 2011). Julia's chapter explores how her family history is related to her PhD journey. The strength of her grandparents to settle in the UK and persist in a country that was explicitly hostile to them has manifested in new ways: Julia's access to spaces and knowledge that were previously inaccessible to her ancestors. More recent initiatives have also aimed to make knowledge and learning more accessible outside the traditional gatekeepers of education (Free Black University, Free Books Campaign).

As April-Louise explores in her chapter, the power exerted and gained through the PhD journey can be used to further support our communities and challenge systems that create these inequalities in the first place. However, while individual and group persistence can lead to some positive change, there are obvious limitations on being able to truly build equity in systems that are structurally anti-Black. As April-Louise describes, the closer Black scholars get to power within academia, the more their mere presence becomes a threat to the status quo, and therefore the more difficult it becomes to navigate these institutions. How do Black scholars persist in these systems without becoming compliant with the anti-Blackness present? This conflict can never be fully resolved in our existing institutions, and many scholars must grapple with the benefit of staying in places that can provide resources, opportunities and reward, with the reality that contributing to these systems, even while explicitly challenging them, can further entrench their power (Joseph-Salisbury & Connelly, 2021).

It is clear from the chapters in this part that Black scholars are resilient and driven by internal motivation – both of which are necessary to complete the arduous challenge of a PhD. However, this internal strength is supplemented by support from many different avenues (as explored in parts III and IV). Without a robust set of support systems, it becomes much harder to overcome the barriers along the PhD journey. Indeed, harassment, bullying and exclusion have been suggested as reasons some Black scholars leave academic roles (Arday, 2022; Gibney, 2022). This holistic view of a scholar's journey is in sharp contrast to the 'lone genius' and individualistic ideology that academic systems perpetuate, where White scholars are often heralded as unique and irreplaceable, while Black scholars are often invisibilised, and Black communities treated as subjects rather than experts of their own cultures and knowledge.

Many Black scholars experience self-doubt despite their hard work and achievements. Indeed, Barbara, Julia, and the author the author of 'I came all this way for this?!' all describe how structural inequalities and interpersonal microaggressions have challenged their self-belief. Job precarity, highly competitive environments, and poor compensation are known to disproportionately impact Black, Asian and minority ethnic academics (Arday, 2017) and, for migrant scholars, these aspects are even more significant (Zewolde, 2021). In 'I came all this way for this?!', the author reflects on the emotional toll of trying to find job opportunities while navigating restrictive immigration policies.

Taking into account the struggles noted above, completing a PhD as a Black scholar is truly an incredible achievement. However, this cannot be fully understood without recognising the broader histories, contributions and traditions of Black communities. It is also clear that, while these achievements are a cause for celebration, it is also a prompt to be critical of the systems that continue to place barriers in the way of many Black scholars.

References

Andrews, K.N. (2011). *Back to Black: Black radicalism and the supplementary school movement* (Doctoral dissertation, University of Birmingham).

Arday, J. (2017). *Exploring black and minority ethnic (BME) doctoral students' perceptions of an academic career*. London: University and College Union.

Arday, J. (2022). 'No one can see me cry: understanding mental health issues for Black and ethnic minority academic staff in higher education', *Higher Education*, 83(1), 79–102. https://doi.org/10.1007/s10734-020-00636-w.

Coard, B. (1971). *How the West Indian child is made educationally subnormal in the British school system: the scandal of the Black child in schools in Britain*. London: New Beacon Books.

Gibney, E. (2022). 'How UK science is failing on diversity', *Nature*. https://www.nature.com/immersive/d41586-022-04386-w/index.html.

Joseph-Salisbury, R. and Connelly, L. (2021). *Anti-racist scholar-activism*. Manchester: Manchester University Press. https://doi.org/10.7765/9781526157973 (accessed 18 September 2023).

Zewolde, S. (2021). *Racism and othering in international higher education: experiences of Black Africans in England.* Oxford: Centre for Global Higher Education, Department of Education, University of Oxford. https://www.researchcghe.org/perch/resources/publications/working-paper-62.pdf (accessed 21 September 2023).

24

What it means to be the first: my journey from Windrush to PhD

Julia Morris

In 1950, my grandad boarded the SS *Castel Verde* at Port Royal, Jamaica. Two months later he arrived in England. Fast forward 70 years and here I am, the first person in our lineage to be awarded a PhD. Throughout the years I have experienced a lot of firsts. During the final year of my undergraduate degree, I applied for a range of PhD projects, which I mainly found on findaPhD.com. I utilised the resources that I had – the university careers service, my personal tutor, and my family. I chose my PhD project based on my passion for the project; however, if I could go back and do things again I would be more cognisant of the institution and supervisory team to which I was applying. I struggled through my PhD mentally, emotionally and academically. After suddenly losing my grandfather to cancer in my second year, I felt lost and broken. Imposter syndrome followed me around like a dark cloud. However, thankfully, I pushed my way through with help from my support system consisting of close family and friends. Almost one year since defending my thesis, I can look back and appreciate the journey.

When my paternal grandfather, Joseph Morris, left the sunny isles of Jamaica aboard the SS *Castel Verde* at Port Royal in May 1950, he was a teenager and one of the first from his area to embark on such a journey. In July he arrived in Southampton, UK, to a hostile and unfamiliar cold. For the first time in his life, he beheld the 'mother country'. This is the story of just one of my grandparents. He, my maternal grandfather, Manzie Buchanan, and grandmothers, Gloria Morris and Pansy Samuels, faced many unknowns and difficulties coming to England from Jamaica in the 1950s and 1960s, but their bravery and perseverance made a way for me. My parents, Bernard and Maureen Morris, were born in the UK in the 1960s. They met and married in the 1980s and had three children, of which I am the youngest.

From the ages of 3–18 I was schooled in White-majority environments. I have always felt different as a result. I was too 'White' for the Black kids but obviously still very much a brown-skinned girl from a British Jamaican household. As I progressed through my schooling career, I learned to care less about fitting in. Through the help of family, friends and mentors, I learned to embrace that I was both Black and nerdy.

I loved science (particularly biology and chemistry) in school and was first introduced to the idea of a PhD by my teacher Dr Hill, as a GCSE student (age 14). He explained the path it took for him to get his doctorate. From those early conversations I knew I had to do well in my GCSEs, study mathematics and at least another science A-level and do well in them. I learned that I then had to get an undergraduate degree, potentially a master's degree, and then finally try to get onto a PhD degree programme. Although no one I knew closely had trodden the path before, I held onto the loose plan my teacher gave.

I went on to do well in my GCSEs and A-levels and was later accepted into the University of Bristol to study Cellular and Molecular Medicine. An opportunity arose during the third year of my degree to participate in an industrial placement, which I seized with both hands. I found during this year that I loved working in the lab, managing experiments and participating in scientific discussion. I wanted to do this full time. During this year I discovered more about the academic pathway. The idea of pursuing a career in science became less of a far-off dream and more of a reality.

In my field, PhD opportunities are advertised by project. Upon return to university for my final year, I applied for a range of PhD projects, which I mainly found on findaPhD.com. I told my family, friends and university colleagues that I was going to apply for PhD projects in a specific area (DNA repair); so they also sent me PhD project adverts. I look back on this with fondness; it exemplifies the power of community. I applied for PhD projects with competitive funding or projects that already came with funding.

Writing PhD applications was a very interesting process. At first, I learned through trial and error. Later, however, I learned to utilise the resources that I had – the university careers service, my personal tutor, scientists I met through my industrial placement year, and people who I was loosely connected who were working towards their PhDs.

After a few 'I am very sorry to inform you that you have not been selected for interview' emails, I received an invitation to interview! I felt excited, but I quickly realised that this was another hurdle I had to overcome. I had no idea how to prepare for a PhD interview! So once again I sought help, particularly from the university careers service. I asked them to do a mock interview, which was very helpful. My university personal tutor also served as a great help. The interview itself was nerve-wracking, but I am thankful for the preparation I had. Following the interview, I received an offer, which I accepted. I graduated from my undergraduate degree in July 2015 and began my PhD studies in October 2015.

The transition between my undergraduate degree and PhD was quite stark. The access to and time for student societies was dramatically reduced. And, of course, I interacted with even fewer people who looked like me on a day-to-day basis. I recall attending a departmental induction in the first week of my PhD. I arrived at a familiar scene, where I was one of two Black people in the room. I remember excitedly thinking to myself: 'wow, there's two of us'.

I chose my PhD project based on my interest and passion for the project, as I wanted to ensure that I stayed interested throughout the duration of the PhD (which, thankfully, I did). However, if I could go back and do things again, I would definitely be more cognisant that the advertised project is not the be-all and end-all of the PhD. Projects are dynamic; they evolve and adapt as time progresses.

My main support through my PhD were my family, friends and the wider church community. I found the distance between where I was studying and my core support system difficult. There are many things that I wish I had known before embarking on my PhD. I would have managed my expectations before starting regarding my relationship with my supervisory team. At first, I likened my PhD supervisors to an undergraduate personal tutor. That, in fact, was not the case; they were there to help keep the project on track.

A PhD is difficult for anyone to navigate. It is, of course, academically rigorous; however, it is also a test of endurance. Throughout my four years of study, I faced physical, mental, emotional and relational challenges – particularly, as I mentioned earlier, after suddenly losing my paternal grandfather to cancer in my second year. Like a marathon runner, there were times during my PhD where I hit walls. I wanted to give up; however, my love of science and my desire to make an impact on the world kept me from doing so.

As a Black person, I found navigating the PhD journey had an extra layer of complexity. I learned a lot on the fly. I made mistakes and learned from them. A recurring problem I found was that no one really understood how I felt. At the time I didn't know anyone who looked like me who had walked this path. Although 2020 was a tremendously difficult year (for a plethora of reasons), I'm glad that many Black academics around the world are now becoming increasingly more visible. I am forever grateful for the connections I have made through Twitter – I am not alone and there are others who feel exactly the way I do!

I passed my PhD viva in November 2019 and was extremely thankful to start my first postdoctoral scientist position in January 2020. Despite earning my PhD I still very much grapple with imposter syndrome. Confounded with this, like many Black academics, I am a first generation doctor and there are often times where I still feel like I don't belong. Mindless comments from people like "oh you're a scientist?", "you work there?", "you've got a PhD?" remind me that wrong assumptions are made about me before I can even open my mouth. Sometimes these comments get to me. However, I am learning to let them go as quickly as they come. Every day I *choose* to believe that I belong. I am pushing my way through with help from my support system consisting of close family and friends. Over a year since defending my thesis,

I can look back and appreciate the journey it took to get here. I am thankful that the scientific community is a multicultural environment and I hope to see more people who look like me working beside me in future.

As I reflect on my (relatively short) life thus far, I realise that I've experienced a lot of firsts. I have often felt frustrated that I couldn't talk science with my family or peers who looked like me, but I never thought of myself as a trailblazer. I've just been in pursuit of doing what I love. I've had to learn things the hard way, and I've made many mistakes along my journey.

To you, reader, I hope my story encourages you to understand that simply being the first of your peers or family should never prevent you from pursuing your goals.

25

Why the 'P' in PhD stands for (Black) Power

April-Louise Pennant

Counternarrative storytelling is an invaluable technique when centering overlooked voices and experiences of race and gender, as seen within theoretical frameworks such as Critical Race Theory and Black feminist epistemology. Additionally, the oral traditions of many African diasporic cultures necessitates storytelling as a crucial component of the sharing and passing down of practices, beliefs and teachings. Storytelling is an art form that can be used as entertainment, within music and in writing. To honour the power and beauty of this custom, I will utilise storytelling to describe what completing a PhD felt like to me.

Learning how to swim

Completing a PhD is akin to being a weak swimmer but being thrown into the deep end of a huge pool, having to learn, right there and then, how to keep yourself from drowning and to eventually be able to swim to the other end. You might have people on the sides of the pool in the stands, let us say friends or family members, who love you and are just as frightened as you, watching you struggle in the water. They will try to offer assistance by shouting out to you to 'keep moving your arms and legs', but they will never be able to understand how deep the water is or just how hard you are trying to keep moving your arms and legs!

Gaining a PhD denotes being part of a tiny group of 1.4 per cent of 25–64-year-olds in the UK that have one (Coldron, 2019). Unfortunately, this tiny percentage has not been broken down further to illustrate what this looks like when accounting for specific characteristics like race, gender and/or social class. But to gain an idea about how many Black British students progress to studying at PhD level, data from United Kingdom Research and Innovation (UKRI) is useful. According to UKRI data, between 2016 and 2019, 'of the total 19,868 PhD funded studentships awarded by UKRI research councils collectively, 245 (1.2 per cent) were awarded to Black or Black Mixed students, with just 30 of those being from Black Caribbean backgrounds' (Williams et al., 2019). So, it is no surprise that, at the beginning, I classed myself as a 'weak swimmer' in the deep end of a huge pool, where the water I was paddling was (patriarchal) Whiteness – a chasm of a pre-existing, socially constructed entity that permeates every nook and cranny. As a Black British woman, I had to enter and successfully learn how to 'swim' and navigate the pool to graduate.

Pool-side coaching

*Then, after what will seem like ages, other people appear at the head of the pool, at the other end to you. These people are your supervisors, mentors, possibly more experienced peers who come and go and take it in turns to tell you **how** to move your arms and legs, and **how** to breathe as you continue to struggle to keep your head above the water. They may even throw you a life buoy. You follow their instructions, and you begin to get the hang of a nice doggy paddle. But, just when you think you have got the hang of it, someone switches on the wave machine and you are hit by wave after wave of water. Then, someone who you cannot see throws in beach balls, which glide into you and cause you to panic. You remember the instructions you were given to keep yourself from going under.*

Whiteness is embedded within the very foundations of the entire education system, as manifested in the structures, the policies and the curriculum (Pennant, 2020a). In this way, the higher a Black person progresses within it, the deeper the pool water gets, and the harder it is to 'swim' due to how close they are venturing into the 'heart of whiteness' (Casey, 1993). In order to survive, they must learn to 'swim' with minimal support, prone to unexpected (sometimes) deliberate obstacles being thrown in their way. And while it may feel like they are just managing to keep their head above the water, they are actually 'engag[ing] with whiteness while simultaneously working to dismantle it' (Leonardo, 2002). Luckily for me, I had many 'poolside coaches' who were significant in my journey, particularly Black women mentors with PhDs who had therefore mastered swimming and who helped me as well. The presence of a Black student at PhD level disrupts the continuity of the 'water' flow in the space. If they are also explicitly centring Blackness in their research, they are intentionally or unintentionally entering into 'a significant site of struggle between the interests and ways of knowing of the West and the interests and ways of resisting of the Other' (Smith, 1999). Through my own experience of disrupting the academic space with my presence, I was able to see how this site of struggle provides new possibilities to reframe Black narratives in ways that have previously been eliminated (Pennant, 2020a).

Finding your feet

Gradually you are able to do various styles of swim strokes, floating slowly, with ease and more confidence around the deep end of the pool. Eventually, you swim and swim and swim, taking any difficulties in your stride. You keep going – although your arms and legs are burning, and you feel like you have no more energy. But you cannot stop because there is a time limit and you have sacrificed so much. So, you keep going until you finally feel the tiling of the pool's floor under your toes first, and then your feet, and you begin to walk in the water, which gets lower and lower on your body. You reach the steps and climb out to the people who have been waiting for you to join them. You are exhausted but excited as you have mastered swimming from the deepest end of this huge pool to the shallowest.

Unfortunately, not every Black person is able to acquire the 'navigational capital' that will provide the 'ability to manoeuvre through institutions not created with communities of colour in mind' (Yosso, 2005). I witnessed many Black students taking leave from their PhDs or quitting altogether because it was just too much. I also cultivated many unconventional strategies (Pennant, 2020b), as well as understanding that it is 'Whiteness' in which

I had to 'swim' and that, by the end of doing so, it would either 'make' or 'break' me. I relished the risk and challenge of being able to withstand the Whiteness until completion – though in hindsight rest and recovery should have been a crucial part of my strategy, particularly during the aftermath of the process. In completing a PhD, I acquired certain advantages, such as being 'privy to some of the most intimate secrets of white society' (Collins, 1986). Secrets that reveal (some of) the unwritten rules embedded within Whiteness, and the very different journey that I have had to take to get to this point – a journey that many of my White counterparts did not have to take. But what I learned at the end of the PhD process was that, as a Black woman, I had gained so much more because I had literally beaten the odds to win an unfair educational steeplechase (Pennant, 2019). Yet many Black students feel frustrated at the end, when many of their non-PhD peers do not understand what they endured to get a PhD and, despite all their additional efforts and credentials, they still may find it difficult to gain full access in the form of secure academic positions (Equality Challenge Unit, 2015). Many will have to venture elsewhere to work in places where their PhD will be undervalued.

And then out of the blue, someone asks you 'why did you do it? And why did it take you soooooo long to get from one end of the pool to the other?' Then another may comment 'it wasn't even that deep!' and another (who probably missed most of the swimming) asks you 'why are you so tired?' And you laugh because you know that not everyone will understand or be able to do what you have just done and that not everyone is supposed to!

What do I wish I knew then that I know now?

What I wish I knew then that I now know, after gaining a PhD myself, is that when you think about a PhD, you should reimagine the 'P' as representing Power, particularly if it is a Black person that has one.

Because being Black with a PhD means using all your power to survive the process.

Because being Black with a PhD means completing your research with the added pressure of 'swimming' within Whiteness.

Because being Black with a PhD means sacrificing a great deal to gain deeper knowledge about your topic and, in the process, yourself.

Because being Black with a PhD means infiltrating the hegemony of White knowledge systems that once excluded your ancestors.

Because being Black with a PhD means assuming a relatively elevated position that will enable you to centre, strategically think upon and support your communities from a unique vantage point.

The famous saying 'knowledge is power' should extend to the notion that the real power is in how one is able to critically apply it. Thus, having a PhD is powerful, as it symbolises one's ability to gain, create and apply knowledge, which is paramount in an increasingly, overt, anti-Black world – a world where intellectual work becomes 'a deadly serious matter', which should transform into 'a practice which always thinks about its intervention in a world in which it would make some difference' (Hall, 1992).

To that end, while there are many roles in the struggle, we as Black communities must encourage, support and include the role of an academic as an important and necessary one within it. If not, the society that separates its scholars from its warriors will have its thinking done by cowards and its fighting done by fools (adapted from quote from Butler, 1889, p. 84).

References

Butler, W.F. (1889). *Charles George Gordon*. London: Macmillan and Co.

Casey, K. (1993). *I answer with my life: life histories of women teachers working for social change*. Abingdon: Routledge.

Coldron, A.C. (2019). 'How rare (or common) is it to have a PhD?'. https://www.findaphd.com/advice/blog/5403/how-rare-or-common-is-it-to-have-a-phd (accessed 30 January 2021).

Collins, P.H. (1986). 'Learning from the outsider within: the sociological significance of Black feminist thought', *Social Problems*, 33(6), S14.

Equality Challenge Unit (2015). 'Academic flight: how to encourage black and minority ethnic academics to stay in UK higher education'. https://www.ecu.ac.uk/wp-content/uploads/2015/03/ECU_Academic-flight-from-UK-education_RR.pdf> (accessed 30 January 2021).

Hall, S. (1992). 'Cultural studies and its theoretical legacies'. In L. Grossberg et al. (eds), *Cultural studies*. London: Routledge, pp. 277–86.

Leonardo, Z. (2002). 'The souls of White folk: critical pedagogy, whiteness studies, and globalization discourse', *Race Ethnicity and Education*, 5(1), 31. https://www.researchgate.net/publication/228851075_The_Souls_of_White_Folk_Critical_Pedagogy_Whiteness_Studies_and_Globalization_Discourse.

Pennant, A.-L. (2019). *"Look, I have gone through the education system and I have tried damn hard to get to where I am, so no one is gonna stop me!": The educational journeys and experiences of Black British women graduates* (Unpublished PhD thesis, University of Birmingham).

Pennant, A. (2020a). 'My journey into the "heart of Whiteness" whilst remaining my authentic (Black) self', *Educational Philosophy and Theory, Special Issue: Exploring the Unequal Space: Race, Social Mobility and Education*, 53(3), 245–56.

Pennant, A. (2020b). '#HowISurvivedMyPhD Twitter thread' September. https://twitter.com/April_LouP/status/1309464899458826240 (accessed 30 January 2021).

Smith, L.T. (1999). *Decolonizing methodologies: research and indigenous peoples*. London: Zed Books Ltd.

Williams, P., Bath, S., Arday, J. and Lewis, C. (2019). *The broken pipeline: barriers to Black PhD students assessing research council funding*. https://leadingroutes.org/the-broken-pipeline (accessed 30 January 2021).

Yosso, T.J. (2005). 'Whose culture has capital? A critical race theory discussion of community cultural wealth', *Race Ethnicity and Education*, 8(1), 69–91.

26

(Un)making the imposter syndrome

Barbara Adewumi

Writing back while Black

The story of my PhD journey can be encapsulated in the following words of the towering author, intellectual and activist Maya Angelou: 'Stand up straight and realise who you are, that you tower over your circumstances' (Angelou, 2014).

I chose to write about my journey of completing my PhD in the hope that I can speak to those who are searching for suggestions on how to stay on course and endure the race to possibly become a Black academic in higher education. When I was planning to do a PhD, I had little knowledge as to how to navigate the rough terrain in accessing funding. I first researched the Economic Social Research Council funding options and soon realised that this highly competitive funding body did not accommodate women like me. After having three children I decided to teach in further education and pursue a PhD. I asked myself, could I realistically secure funding from such an elitist funding system? After weighing up the financial costs, the need to conduct my research became more imminent and I decided to self-fund my PhD. Fortunately, due to my teaching experience, I was employed as an associate lecturer while doing my PhD at the university. In retrospect, I realise how fortunate I was to complete my PhD on a full-time basis. In the current neoliberal climate, it has become exceedingly difficult and exceptionally competitive for Black students to gain

PhD funding, as many undergraduates attend post-92 universities as opposed to Russell Group universities. From my experience, a self-funded PhD requires self-discipline, tenacity and mental strength to keep going through the ebbs and flows of the PhD journey. Despite being frugal with my research budget, I was continually existing on an overdraft, but I did not let that deter me. Past studies have shown that many Black PhD students are forced to do their PhD part time and work numerous jobs as well as struggle with the burden of teaching.

During my second year, I had no other option but to take on additional paid work by teaching part time in a nearby further education college as well as teaching part time at the university. The experience was both mentally and physically exhausting, as days merged into nights, preparing lectures and seminars, marking, and writing chapters for my PhD. My family life was timed to military precision that barely allowed sleep! For some time, I was burning the candle at both ends, and it was the hardest thing I had to do. But I insisted on being a role model for my daughters and could not fold under the pressure. Caribbean women in my family taught me to endure difficult situations to better the lives of those we preciously nurture who will follow on from us. 'There is no force equal to a woman determined to rise', so goes the saying often attributed to W.E.B. Du Bois. Eventually, however, something had to give. The worst feeling was to be preoccupied with money worries while trying to study. This level of study requires creative head space and moments when you need to block out the noise. Luckily, I found out about a small financial aid package offered to students at the university, and so I no longer had to work so many teaching hours. My advice to Black PhD students who are self-funded is to find out whether your university can help support you financially, as there are pockets of funding available. You need to accept that you cannot do it all, and seek assistance.

After a long hot summer, I finally completed my field research. I felt rather out of place having been under the radar for a while with staff and other PhD peers. As months passed, I struggled to find time to access research development opportunities. I observed from the sidelines my White peers presenting at conferences and co-writing with other staff with similar research interests. I began to feel inadequate – questioning my research skills and presence in this academic space. I found it difficult to find spaces that I could occupy confidently. First there was the absence of relevant academic networks, which limited my opportunities academically, coupled with the scarcity of Black academics at my university. A feeling of being invisible developed into an internal discourse of othering; it came to the point where I was always second-guessing myself as to whether I was just an imposter. Reflecting on my marginalised being, author Professor Patricia Hill Collins resonates to my then uncertain positionality within the academy:

> As individuals, each of us occupies a dual location: included in some groups yet excluded from others. The issue for most of us lies in being a pure insider or outsider than in terms of our participation within all of the venues to which we belong. (Hill Collins, 2013: 4)

My advice is to remember you are going towards the unknown and you will need to stretch yourself mentally so you can demonstrate your originality in your field and build your confidence. Once you overcome the battle of self-dialogue, completing a PhD becomes a fulfilling experience.

Four years later, having completed my PhD, I wanted to further develop my skills and pursue an academic research career. As time passed, I faced academic casualisation, and reluctantly agreed to work fixed-term teaching contracts for several years. Such precarious contracts became problematic for me. On the one hand they provided flexibility, juggling work with family. But on the other hand there was no time to publish. A disquieting feeling came over me as I began to embody the notorious fear of publish or perish! To write was a luxury reserved for only the most privileged faculty members as others, like me, were glued to the lower rungs of the academic ladder. Fixed-term contracts prohibited Black early-career researchers from really 'getting on' with writing and developing the craft of successfully publishing. I had this naïve impression that if I did my job exceedingly well, giving over and above what was required, surely the institution would take note. But I was forever waiting in the wings for an opportunity that never seemed to materialise. Shirley Anne Tate so poignantly expresses my feeling of being 'in a location of (un)location and un-belonging' (Gabriel & Tate, 2017). Many emerging BAME academic staff follow this method of resilience as a response to the institution's neoliberal management; however, there is little acknowledgment of the difficult environments within the academic workplace which Black staff have to navigate. Many fear trivialisation, so most tolerate the uncomfortable feelings of being othered. Studies show that Black staff are underrepresented in more senior roles and overrepresented in more junior roles and are more likely to be on fixed-term lower-paid contracts longer than their White counterparts.

One autumn term a new staff member of colour joined the school and we met for lunch to discuss our research. I was invited to present my research at an equality and race conference with her and some other colleagues. This was the first time I had encountered a microaffirmation about my work. Such a fortunate encounter highlights the ongoing struggle for recognition and professional support within White-dominated institutions. As a mature, Black, female, early-career researcher, I have learnt from doing a PhD that you need to find a way to try and fit into the culture of academia and find access to the institution's academic and social capital to gain traction in your career. I recommend you seek advice through external Black academic networks, such as Black British Academics, which provide encouragement and networking to more marginalised academics, and thereby create opportunities for yourself. I suggest you find or create your own support system, such as a mentor, and surround yourself with like-minded friends, staff and academic peers. Think of ways you can build an opportunity for yourself to gain greater exposure in White-dominated academic spaces; for example, arrange to shadow a senior academic at a conference as this is a great way to network.

As one of the very few Black postdoctoral researchers in the university, I have had the privilege to research and publish. In this chapter, my encounters clearly reveal the struggles within oneself to survive and thrive in academia. Framing my experiences through the lens of Critical Race Theory storytelling has been one of self-discovery, as well as a cathartic experience toward (un)making the imposter syndrome that plagued the earlier years of my academic career. I now join with strength and conviction other staff of colour as a collective that act as powerful advocates and vehicles for institutional cultural change towards the progress of Black academics in UK higher education.

References

Angelou, M. (2014). *Rainbow in the cloud: the wisdom and spirit of Maya Angelou.* New York: Random House Publishing Group. https://blackbritishacademics.co.uk/.

Hill Collins, P. (2013). *On intellectual activism.* Philadelphia: Temple University Press.

Gabriel, D. and Tate, S. (2017). *Inside the ivory tower.* London: UCL IOE Press

27

I came all this way for this?! An international student's experience of UK higher education

Anon

A few years ago, I had the satisfaction of watching one of the most powerful, inspiring, and touching speeches I have ever seen. Most probably, the reader will also have seen it, or at least heard about it, as it made the headlines around the world. I am talking about the speech delivered by the American actress Viola Davis after receiving the Emmy award for best leading actress in 2015. She began her speech quoting Harriet Tubman, who stated the following in the 1800s:

> In my mind, I see a line. And over that line, I see green fields and lovely flowers and beautiful White women with their arms stretched out to me over that line, but I cannot seem to get there no-how. I cannot seem to get over that line.

Viola Davis then complemented this by saying: 'Let me tell you something. The only thing that separates women of colour from anyone else is opportunity. You cannot win an Emmy for roles that are not there.'

Bringing this powerful speech into the context of the present essay is not only important but also highly pertinent, as its key theme intertwines with the scope of my personal account: the opportunity to display one's value, skills, knowledge, competence and potential. In the specific case of an academic career, without egalitarian opportunities it is impossible to cross the line preventing Black scholars from ever standing before a university classroom and/or conducting research. Thus, in this essay, I present my perceptions and experience of trying to cross this line to reach the 'green field' of academia, which seems increasingly out of reach for Black scholars.

I am a Black man who arrived in the UK in 2014 from a developing country with the clear and well-defined goal of becoming an international-level social science researcher and lecturer. Within the timeframe of a year and a half prior to arriving in the country, I had applied to eight competitive programmes and was accepted for six. Achieving such a high success rate brought me great joy and satisfaction. It is well-known that, like the USA, the UK has an enduring and strong reputation for providing world-class education, especially at PhD level, along with a solid tradition of developing influential and high-impact research across a variety of disciplines. Moreover, UK universities are also regarded as spaces fostering a rich academic environment comprising a diverse cohort of scholars and students from many countries. Consequently, my choice to come to the UK was consistent with this scenario and, most importantly, with my long-term career goal.

Although I successfully completed my PhD in Sociology within four years, like numerous other PhD candidates this was not without overcoming a number of challenging situations and difficulties. Examples include: a lack of funding, as I did not have a scholarship; the language barrier, given that English is not my first language; establishing a track record of publications during the PhD; gaining teaching experience; and finding the right balance between personal life and research demands.

But do not get me wrong, I certainly do not want to claim that I was caught completely by surprise; neither did I believe that the PhD journey would be completely smooth and hassle-free. I was aware that I would encounter some obstacles here and there along the way. However, I thought that, once I graduated, I would receive some genuine opportunities to start my academic career and put those tough moments behind me. Regrettably, however,

I was wrong. I had not realised that the greatest stumbling block was still to come. Trying to enter UK academia has proved to be a virtual mission impossible, whether as a teaching fellow, research assistant, postdoctoral fellow, or any other fancy title for entry-level positions. The plain fact is that there seems to be a thick and rigid line, albeit invisible, that is virtually impossible for Black people to cross. This is probably even more the case for international PhD graduates like me, despite having graduated from a Russell Group university that, in theory, is supposed to carry some sort of seal of excellence regarding one's degree. In reality, it does not make any difference.

On top of this, I have also learnt by experience and by talking to several other male and female Black peers that, regrettably, the careers services of most UK universities are not yet prepared to provide specialised support for Black PhD students to succeed in academic job hunting. This is even more problematic for international students who, for example, need support in understanding the possibilities of receiving sponsorship to obtain a working visa, how to prepare for an interview, and how to make sense of the academic salary grade system, benefits, pensions, and so forth. Quite often, when you approach careers services requesting a more specific form of support or consultation, they simply give you a list of websites to look at and nothing else. At the end of the day, you are on your own, which is very disappointing.

For some years in UK academia, there have been voices asking: 'Why isn't my professor Black?' If you Google this search query, you will find dozens of articles and video recordings of roundtables addressing this topic. What I can say about this issue is that, after my experience in attempting to pass through the astonishingly narrow and selective door of UK academia, the answer to this pertinent and relevant question seems clear. There are no (or very few) Black professors in UK universities because we are not given egalitarian opportunities. This is what was said by Viola Davis back in 2015 and before her, with different words, by Harriet Tubman in the 1800s, by W.E.B. Du Bois in 1903, and countless other Black men and women thereafter. Opportunity (or the lack of it) does make all the difference!

Most UK universities claim that they foster equal employment opportunities and strongly encourage members of underrepresented ethnic groups to apply. In fact, I have to say that the first few times I read this kind of statement in job advertisements and application forms I was genuinely amazed, because in my country of origin it is not common for employers to openly adopt this sort of approach. In fact, they prefer not to compromise themselves so that they can continue to foster White privileges without being challenged. Thus, reading equal employment opportunity statements does make one believe that you have a fair chance of succeeding in your application. It conveys the idea that one's academic credentials and achievements, competence, experience and potential will be fairly assessed and seriously considered.

Nevertheless, further down the road, and after having so many doors closed in your face, you start to wonder whether, in reality, this equal opportunity claim represents more of a nice façade than actual practice. After all, if this claim genuinely reflected everyday practice, there would not be so many voices asking why their professor is not Black. Moreover, a recent study, published in early 2021, reveals that ethnic minorities are more likely to be out of work because employers are rejecting job applications from people whose names suggest they are non-White (Zwysen & Di Stasio, 2021) and, I would add, non-British. Besides, a previous study revealed that of the 13,500 professors in the UK, only 85 were Black (that is, 0.63 per cent) (Bhopal, 2018). Consequently, these findings represent strong evidence testifying that I am not the only one noticing that something seems to be out of place in UK academia.

Furthermore, as an applicant, you are always left completely in the dark in the sense that feedback is never provided, even though application processes are extremely demanding and both time and energy-consuming. The complete absence of any sort of feedback to applicants after an unsuccessful application makes it even more challenging for recent Black PhD graduates to understand what they can do to improve their profile, what their strengths and weaknesses are, and so on. To provide such feedback is not patronising but respectful and considerate to emerging scholars.

Talking about this issue with an experienced and well-established professor, I was told that it is a common and natural practice to not provide feedback because 'nobody has time to do that'. However, I have to say this did not make me feel any better. In fact, I consider it quite unfortunate to hear this kind of justification because it implies that my time is less valuable and important than theirs. In other words, it is perfectly fine if I spend several hours and weeks putting together a good application package, writing countless versions of research proposals and statements, asking busy professors to provide reference letters and then following these up to ensure they do so within the deadline. However, all the tremendous effort and energy behind this work does not appear to be worth any kind of feedback, apart from a standard short message telling me that I was not shortlisted. Ultimately, from my point of view, the process becomes more of an immense guessing game rather than providing egalitarian employment opportunities for early-career Black scholars.

Finally, I think it is important to state that I do not ask for pity or commiseration with my account. Neither did Viola Davis, or any other Black professional. Instead, I just wish that the opportunities could really be as fair and egalitarian as most UK universities claim. It might indeed look quite appealing and catchy in their institutional brochure and advertisements to say that they foster diversity and so forth. But, regrettably, a somewhat different reality has been shown in academic classrooms for many years. And well-qualified emerging Black scholars such as I are the living proof of that.

References

Bhopal, K. (2018). 'Black academics feel they must be twice as good', *Network*, 130, 34–5.

Zwysen, W. and Di Stasio, V. (2021). 'Ethnic minorities are more likely to be unemployed because employers reject applications from "non-white" names', *British Sociological Association*. https://www.britsoc.co.uk/media-centre/press-releases/2020/december/ethnic-minorities-more-likely-to-be-unemployed-because-employers-reject-applications-from-non-white-names/.

Reflections on Part V and prompts for action

Madina Wane

It is clear that the journeys of Black PhD students are shaped by a huge number of factors within and beyond education. Accounts in this part have highlighted the many obstacles facing Black students, but also the areas for improvement, and the power of community action. As an educator, parent or any other community or institutional member, where do you think change can be made?

Many of us strive for equitable change and increased opportunities for Black students. However, in the meantime, students continue to enter a system that is hostile to them. How do we balance being honest with students about the struggles in progression and precarity in academia, without deterring them from potential opportunities? Are there any actions that are needed alongside these conversations?

Conclusion and recommendations

De-Shaine Murray

Twenty-seven personal accounts, 27 unique stories, 27 lessons to be learned. In the five preceding parts of this book, you have read the stories of Black academics across the UK, who have detailed their experiences of aspiring to and obtaining a PhD degree. From the perils and pitfalls of being Black and applying for a PhD in Part I, to the reflections at the completion of a PhD journey in Part V, the challenges and difficulties Black PhD scholars face have been outlined in their own words. These accounts speak to the resilience, determination and ingenuity that has led them to succeed in spite of their academic environments. The chapters have spoken of personal struggles for rights and recognition after entering white academic spaces (in Part II). They also detail the innovative Black support networks that have filled institutional voids, often at a great cost to already marginalised individuals (Part III). We have also seen instances in Part IV where supervisors, programmes and departments have provided exceptional support that has facilitated the success of Black students. These accounts, written between 2021 and 2023, stand as a collective testimony of the current state of UK academia for Black people undertaking doctoral research.

Consistent themes

From Part I of the book, focusing on students applying to study for a PhD, issues of *access*, *lack of information*, *uncertainty*, *confidence* and *isolation* consistently appear. From these accounts, we can see that the path to a PhD is often mystifying, inaccessible and prohibitively difficult to understand. Where do you find PhD places? Do you contact supervisors beforehand? Is joining a centre for doctoral training the best decision for me? The path to a PhD is not uniform and needs to be better explained to those looking to be admitted. More needs to be done to inform Black undergraduates and master's students about PhD research, in regards to the requirements for study, the opportunities available and the benefits that can be accrued. How can we expect Black students to undertake this qualification if there is no complete and definitive picture of what a PhD entails? The onus must be placed on institutions and funding bodies, to consistently reach out to schools, communities and current students, to build bridges that provide students with accessible pathways to the next stages of their academic development.

These pathways must also consider the various intersections of Black students, developing best practices that account for the diversity within our community – we are not a monolith. As documented in various chapters in this book, unique experiences of academia can be had due to the interplay of race with gender, class, cultural background, disability, immigration status, neurodiversity and religion. We are comprised of multiple identities that shape our world view and how we are perceived and ultimately treated by others. A Black woman's navigation of academia can differ greatly from that of their male counterparts, having to deal with a distasteful cocktail of both racism and sexism. The needs of a first-generation migrant may not be the same as a scholar whose grandparents came to the UK as part of the Windrush generation. Language barriers may be a consideration and there may be varying levels of familial support. The considerations for a Black neurodiverse scholar could be different to that of someone neurotypical, and the experiences of a Black scholar who is of low income and the first in their family to attend university can differ dramatically from somebody whose parents are well acquainted with academia. Therefore, outreach and interventional programmes must be well informed on the nuances found within our community, while addressing the underlying thread that unites these journeys – racism within academia and higher education.

Our focus has been the PhD journey, but we recognise that this journey starts not in the university but in schools, families

Conclusion and recommendations

and communities. Early educational experiences, both positive and negative, can have a lasting impact on the trajectory of Black scholars. In aiming to understand how we can improve as a sector, Black children need to be inspired, developed and informed of all the possible routes they can take. Wraparound structures that empower and support both students and their families at all stages will ensure that those who may not be acquainted with structures can interact with educational systems and be prepared for future study and attainment if they choose. Many of our contributors made reference to their early years and pivotal moments that guided their paths. We collectively need to ensure that the racism, discrimination, stereotypes and adultification that Black kids disproportionately face in our education system are eradicated. Black children need the space to dream, the resources to thrive, and the paths to become the academics of tomorrow.

Given the high numbers of Black people who come from disadvantaged backgrounds, it is difficult for us to actively encourage Black students to undertake a PhD if it puts them into financial difficulty. The Runnymede report, *The colour of money* (Khan, 2020) found that for every £1 of White British wealth, Black Caribbean households on average have 20 pence and Black African households have ten pence. This is further exacerbated by the cost-of-living crisis. Studying for a PhD after undergraduate debt and possibly master's loans is a prohibitively expensive endeavour. Many Black students cannot support themselves or their families while undertaking this qualification. A PhD studentship remunerates less than most graduate jobs and many cannot afford to continue in further study if they cannot afford to live. These barriers also persist at earlier stages. If master's qualifications are a prerequisite for PhD acceptance, more scholarships and studentships are needed to ensure that students do not incur financial trouble, having to take out loans or work part-time jobs in order to progress. These barriers to entry and success need to be removed or further study will remain solely the pursuit of those who can afford it.

However, to boil these issues down to just financial struggles is a gross simplification. Our text has demonstrated that the barriers facing Black students are multifaceted and, even for those who are successful, it comes at a price. Why would a Black student want to continue in or enter an institution that does not even remotely resemble them? How can we encourage persistence and resilience in environments that are actively knocking their confidence? The severe underrepresentation and exclusion, referenced in many chapters, leads to isolation, where students feel that they 'don't 'fit in'. In these experiences the words 'exhausted', 'tired', 'fed up' and 'disillusioned' frequent the pages. It seems that successful navigation of these spaces is costly: requiring code switching, ignoring racism, processing microaggressions, and generally having to shed a sense of self and one's identity in order to progress. In addition, students are not seeing representation at higher levels of the academic pipeline, that is Black PhD students, Black postdoctoral researchers, Black lecturers and Black professors, which makes them feel as if progression is not possible. This can manifest in a lack of belonging, deterioration in mental health, a reduction in attainment or terminating their studies altogether. Therefore, to increase the number of Black students that enter, develop and are retained at academic institutions, the environments they frequent across all levels must be reimagined.

Even after these barriers, if a prospective Black PhD student continues on this journey and applies, we see uncertainty and a lack of transparency in the PhD selection process. If recruitment committees are involved, are they representative? Who is ensuring that the selection process is as fair as possible? Why in many instances is there not appropriate feedback for the Black students who have applied and been unsuccessful in their applications? Academic hiring practices at doctoral level can be opaque, lax and subject to bias. The freedom and autonomy afforded to those who make decisions on accepting students also means that scrutiny of processes is underdeveloped. Where scrutiny is deficient or non-existent, there is room for discrimination to occur. There needs to be a rethink about how PhD students are hired, that is more uniform and transparent. There is no secret that people recruit in their own image. In the sciences many research groups have a dominant culture that reflects the background and identity of the principal investigator. If Black students do not have the personal connections to academics, do not know how to reach out, or are not represented at the highest level, they will not be able to progress. In these spaces who you know is just as important as what you know. In addition, whether we like to admit it or not, academia abides by a very specific set of rules, practices and codes that can be hard to grasp for those at the trainee stage. What you know can sometimes be learnt from a book or a Google search; however, there is also a 'hidden curriculum' that is passed down through lessons and teachings by those who have come before you. In the case of prospective Black PhD students, we are often the first of our families and are forced to learn on the job, as we grow through academia. These lessons are not always easy to find and can be uncomfortable to learn. There can also be greater consequences as a Black scholar for getting things wrong within the academy, where failure to follow unspoken rules can lead to further bias, discrimination and racism. Guidance and mentorship is therefore needed to help students get acclimatised to the distinct way in which academic spaces operate, in addition to hopefully changing the toxicity and hypercompetitive culture that permeates higher education.

Upon entering the academy, many Black PhD students find themselves in a battle, fighting for changes on multiple levels. The middle portion in this collection of accounts has shown the individual battles that Black scholars have faced, when researching topics that challenge the very fabric of established, academic principles. They say history is written by the winners and academia in many fields has a prevailing homogeneous voice that oftentimes has a very myopic (Eurocentric, colonial and Global North dominated) view of the world. Our admittance within these spaces can lead to a broadening and enriching of our fields, with viewpoints and ideas being incorporated that were previously excluded. This process, however, can lead to tension, contention and backlash. Including Black scholarship within academia benefits all parties, but is frequently met with resistance, as seen in Part II. Diversity among academics can provide a more accurate view of history, lead to the creation of inclusive tools, push the proliferation of scientific breakthroughs that have a wider impact and catalyse the development of imaginative art that provides transformative change. There is room for all of us, and our contributions and our inclusion will only enhance academic research.

Our accounts have also touched on the battles that have led to mobilisation through the creation of collectives. Building community in response to adversity is a common theme from many of our contributors; it most prominently features in the accounts found in Part III but also throughout the book. It must be further examined why higher education is so hostile to Black students, that many are forced to respond to conflict with their peers, supervisors and departments. Within these experiences, a clear sense of activism emerges, where Black students hold a conflicting position trying to progress through structures that are oppressive in nature. Despite this, many beautiful support networks have blossomed, filling institutional gaps and providing the community and guidance that many of us crave. Such organising is bittersweet, where trainees who have to navigate their own research and development within academia are tasked with strengthening their peers and carrying out the 'academic housework' of more senior scholars. This is a minority tax that burdens many Black trainees, who are not able to solely focus on their research. Such leadership under pressure is often not a choice, where Black scholars attempt to reconfigure structures that seem skewed to our disadvantage. We unequivocally believe that this burden should stop. Institutions must bear the weight of supporting the Black students they have recruited. The attrition that we see at this level is directly influenced by the shortcomings of many institutions that seem woefully ill-equipped to protect, support and lift up their Black scholars and sufficiently support the extra work that some Black students juggle.

However, it would be remiss of us to not acknowledge those who have understood the assignment and been active in their allyship and support. Part IV shows examples of PhD scholars who were built up by their programmes, supervisors and departments – sometimes in very difficult circumstances. There were proactive interventions, conflict resolution and advocacy that allowed scholars to focus solely on what they came to academia to do – conduct research. To the supervisors, administrators and departments that have treated, and continue to treat, Black students with the humanity and dignity they deserve, we say thank you. This should be the baseline, common practice and not something that Black PhD students should have to beg for. Many of us have had to reach breaking point, either physically or mentally, before we were afforded the care and protections from our institutions and, even then, many do not get the appropriate help and subsequently fall through the cracks. We acknowledge those within the system who do good but are aware that this is not the norm within UK higher educational spaces. If we want Black scholars to thrive within our system and stay within academia, we must make these experiences a rule, not an exception.

Upon the completion of a PhD, many Black scholars feel an immense sense of pride after enduring their degree and making it to the end, but often sustain battle scars that stay with them. Many of us feel as if we have survived a process, where we have had to 'swim through the deep end' and push against academia's distinctive hegemony. Gaining a PhD as a Black scholar is a triumph but also often a marathon that is run with a multitude of obstacles. The contributors who spoke of their feelings after becoming a doctor of philosophy mentioned the difficulty of belonging within academia, the lack of recognition for them as Black PhD earners and the lack of understanding (at times) from our communities about the feat they had accomplished. In addition, being a Black PhD recipient does not discount you from ongoing racism and bias that halts further progression. The fact that Royal Society statistics place the percentage of Black UK scholars at the postdoctoral level who would be eligible for their remit at approximately 1 per cent shows a continuation of this problem (Royal Society, 2021). In addition, United Kingdom Research and Innovation diversity data in 2021 showed that the percentage of Black principal investigator grant holders was also 1 per cent and the award rate was 13 per cent, significantly lower than the award rates for White (29 per cent) and Asian academics (23 per cent). Even if Black PhD students do not know these statistics, they feel the effect of them in their everyday journeys, experiences and wider prospects. Reform must therefore be enacted across all levels, from bright-eyed undergraduate to distinguished professor, if we are truly serious about Black inclusion in UK higher education.

Ultimately, this book provides an honest account of the Black PhD experience, the one that escapes the open days, website pictures and glossy prospectuses. We are frank about the realities of being Black in the academy, not to deter Black participation but to light the path. We want Black students and trainees to be equipped with the right tools to succeed in these spaces. There is no clearer way to aid this than to learn from the experiences shared in this book and act accordingly. Although shining a light on the Black PhD experience may reveal a lot of dirt and uncomfortable truths, we believe this is an opportunity to clean, correct and change our academic practices to ensure that Black scholars can thrive. This work must be undertaken collaboratively, with effective input from the dominant group. There have been more than enough articles, reports and statistics that have provided evidence to substantiate the accounts shared by our contributors. Now we demand sustained action.

A change is gonna come ... right?

Looking at one component of Critical Race Theory, interest convergence, we see that the strides of a marginalised group toward racial equality may only be successful when it coincides with a vested interest of the dominant group – in this instance Black people and White people (Bell, 1980; Driver, 2011; Rollock & Gillborn, 2011).

For many, the question of when change will come has remained unanswered for decades. When employing interest convergence as a framework of analysis, it can be argued that an improvement to the experiences of marginalised students is simply not a priority for the oppressive majority. The question we ask is, what is this hypothetical 'vested interest' where racial equity within academia is concerned? And is it enough to see a proactive commitment?

As many of the chapters have highlighted, a lot of work done recently (following the Black Lives Matter movement of 2020) has been born out of a delayed and dampened guilt that sees institutions make changes out of fear of retribution – not compassion. If the disdain of the Black community was a powerful enough motivator, institutions, both higher education and beyond, would have made these changes long before 2020, and George Floyd may still be breathing. It is important to recognise that real change will not come to many institutions so long as they continue to see contributions made by Black academics as less than that of White academics. Similarly, progress will remain superficial so long as the power held by these institutions is not interrogated and redistributed more equitably.

So, invariably, the next question that should be asked is where do we go from here? What should be done to include, build up and empower Black British academics and researchers?

Areas for action

Although we believe that the sharing of these experiences is powerful in its own right and should provide ample inspiration for universities and funding bodies to make appropriate changes, there are a few recommendations we would make that will lead to immediate change within our sector. We are certainly not the first and we probably will not be the last to recommend changes to our sector for the advancement of Black students (Alexander and Arday, 2015; Arday, 2017; Williams et al., 2019; Rollock, 2019). However, our collective time within academia has given us some insight into possible areas of action to address a lot of the themes that have been unearthed by the sharing of our stories. There follows a list of actions, derived from each part of this book, that we believe can be taken in order to support, retain and develop Black students.

Bring real transparency and uniformity to the PhD application process

We want Black students to have a fair chance of obtaining PhDs. This will not be possible without removing the opacity of the PhD application process and standardising it across departments, institutions and the country to minimise biases in shortlisting, interviews and selection.

Support for Black students must be proactive

Prioritise the mental health of Black students

Therapy and safe spaces for Black students are a must. While institutions undergo the necessary but often glacial change of becoming anti-racist, Black trainees need access to free and culturally competent mental health support to help them navigate the many hostile environments, cultures and people currently present in higher education.

Effective processes to deal with racism and bullying

Clear, actionable processes are needed for those on the receiving end of racism and bullying. A strength of academic research is the freedom and creativity that can be afforded to those who run research groups. This same power and responsibility must not be abused. Speaking up about mistreatment in the academy can lead to blacklisting and harm for the victim, due to the huge power imbalance between professors and students. Fair, transparent mediation, conflict resolution and, if needed, disciplinary action ensures that Black trainees feel protected and supported by their institutions.

Funding Black support groups – so much work has already been done

Due to historical and current insufficiencies, many Black academics have taken it upon themselves to create networks and communities that support Black students and trainees within their institutions and further afield. This work must be celebrated, supported and uplifted by institutions, with adequate support for those within the community and proper institutional backing to avoid an undue burden on community leaders.

Supervisors, supervisors, supervisors!

Real mentorship

The successes, and equally the failures, of many Black students can boil down to who is charged with their care. Black students need holistic mentorship that does not just view them as labour or a means to an end. This problem is endemic to our sector but takes on a more insidious form when anti-Black racism is included. Black PhD students must be equipped with the right resources to develop and succeed. Supervisors who mentor Black students must adequately educate themselves and act to ensure that they can sufficiently guide and advocate for their Black students.

Clear, regular milestones and checkpoints

PhD research, by definition, can be very isolating. Clear milestones and checkpoints at regular intervals during the process ensure that students are being guided along the right lines. These checkpoints should be conducted by the primary supervisor but also academics who are independent of the trainee's research environment, to ensure that there are proper checks, balances and challenges that can be troubleshooted before they become problems. These checkpoints must also be sufficiently wide-reaching that not just the supervisee but the supervisory environment is also being assessed. If it is found to be unsatisfactory, this verdict must be followed with action.

Demystifying and facilitating what is next, what is my PhD worth?

The PhD process should not be a black box and neither should post-PhD prospects. The attrition in academia for Black individuals continues after the PhD. Demystifying the postdoctoral journey and ascension through levels of lectureship and professorship will help ensure that Black academics are retained. This, coupled with the expansion of funding schemes to transition Black doctoral students to postdoctoral researchers and beyond, will immediately ensure that talented trainees are not lost at transition points within the pipeline. We must also acknowledge that the vast majority of PhD awardees will not stay in academia; therefore, doctoral training programmes and departments should prepare their graduates adequately for the wider world of work.

And while we wait for change

There is a pressing need for a Black academic ecosystem to ensure that Black academics and aspiring Black scholars have spaces that we can call our own. It is alarming that in the twenty-first century in UK academia, White people are still determining what happens to Black students and Black academics at every step of our academic journey. This needs to change. Black people need to be empowered to make decisions that determine our own academic futures and have the mechanisms and resources to ensure we have a continuous pipeline of Black academic development and success. Across the country we need Black interdisciplinary research centres of excellence led by Black academics who are committed to academic excellence, equity and inclusion. We need spaces where Black scholars set research priorities, spaces where Black scholars fund research projects, spaces where Black scholars determine scholarships and fund them, spaces where Black scholars engage with Black communities in the co-creation of knowledge to improve the lived experience of Black people. This is not an alternative to institutions addressing their problems; Black academic empowerment should operate in conjunction with wider higher education institutional reforms on equity and inclusion. #Nothing about us without us.

These points for action scratch the surface of the change needed within UK academia, but we deem them necessary starting points to bring about a future where the barriers for Black scholars are eradicated and we are able to realise our full potential without limit.

References

Alexander, C. and Arday, J. (2015) 'Aiming higher'. https://www.runnymedetrust.org/publications/aiming-higher (accessed 8 May 2024).

Arday, J. (2017) 'Exploring black and minority ethnic (BME) doctoral students' perceptions of a career in academia: experiences, perceptions and career progression'. https://www.ucu.org.uk/media/8633/BME-doctoral-students-perceptions-of-an-academic-career/pdf/JA_BME_doc_students_report_Jun17.pdf (accessed 8 May 2024).

Bell, D. (1980) '*Brown v. Board of Education* and the Interest-Convergence Dilemma', *Harvard Law Review*, 93(3), 518–533.

Driver, J. (2011) 'Rethinking the Interest-Covergence Thesis', *Northwestern University Law Review*, 105(1), 149–197.

Khan, O. (2020) 'The colour of money: how racial inequalities obstruct a fair and resilient economy'. https://www.runnymedetrust.org/publications/the-colour-of-money (accessed 8 May 2024).

Mellors-Bourne, R. (2021) 'The profile of postdoctoral researchers in the UK eligible for Royal Society early career fellowship programmes'. https://royalsociety.org/news-resources/publications/2021/trends-ethnic-minorities-stem/ (accessed 8 May 2024).

Rollock, N. (2019). *Staying power: the career experiences and strategies of UK Black female professors.* London: UCU.

Rollock, N. and Gillborn, D. (2011) 'Critical Race Theory (CRT)', British Educational Research Association online resource. https://www.bera.ac.uk/publication/critical-race-theory-crt (accessed 8 May 2024).

Williams, P., Bath, S., Arday, J. and Lewis, C. (2019). *The broken pipeline: barriers to Black students accessing Research Council funding.* London: Leading Routes.

Our ancestors' wildest dreams ... (fictionalisation)

Jacqueline Darkwa

The following account you are about to read is a fictionalisation. Inspired by the accounts of this text, Cyrus Rose represents an imagined future that centres the Black British higher education experience within a broader African diasporic educational framework, and sees higher education take on a new form. This is a snapshot of what a future Black academic's journey to success could look like.

Cyrus Rose – for my Bibi

Yesterday, I had the opportunity of a lifetime.

I find myself writing this in a hotel room overlooking a setting sun on the coast of the Dar es Salaam.

Yesterday afternoon, I sat in a beautiful room filled with faces, flanked by some of the most brilliant minds of African and Caribbean descent. Invited by a good friend and colleague, I came to sit on a panel to discuss: What does the future of collaborative African-Caribbean research look like in an era of artificial intelligence?

Like myself, all the other panellists are experienced academics and communicators across multiple fields from epidemiology, water science, education and theoretical physics. I, Cyrus Rose, am a marine biologist who has been studying the impact of Islamic East African indigenous ecological practices in reclaiming sea life on the Tanzanian coast.

As a young boy, I used to go back to Tanzania with my family to visit my grandparents. It was my favourite time, especially when my grandmother took me and my sister fishing just off the coast. I loved to hear her speak about all the fish she would catch and fry for dinner, to help her pull in the net and watch the way the fish danced in the boat. It's one of my most treasured memories – by the time I was doing my A-levels the waters of Dar had suffered and my grandmother could no longer fish. The more I think about it, the clearer it is to me that those memories made me the marine conservationist I am today.

I chose to study biology at my university in the north east of England because they had great teachers and were a sister university to an institution in Dar es Salaam. This provided me with opportunities to study in my country of origin. When I got accepted onto my MRes in Marine Biology, my grandmother was the first person I told. A picture of us on her boat in the Indian Ocean was the background to my laptop, a visual motivator during the late nights of lab work and analysis.

During my MRes, I became a member of the Afro-Caribbean Society, hosting networking events for postgraduate and postdoctoral scholars. One transformational doctoral student I met was Lisa, a London-born St Lucian and Guyanese. She was in the second year of her studies in the field of Anthropology and Archival. She and I became fast friends, and she suggested that I volunteer for the student festival where all university students get the chance to set up a stall to engage the university and the public with their work. I turned elements of my research into video content in Swahili to share with my friends and family back home, but most importantly to share with my grandmother – she was so excited to hear about my work in our mother tongue. I almost cried!

During the festival, I met a professor who would become my PhD supervisor. He was half Eritrean and understood my passion for home. He introduced me to academics working in similar fields across the world and encouraged me to consider doctoral studies. His guidance and support was fundamental to my PhD experience. I was able to source financial support from both the Marine Biological Association and the British Council's Reparatory Justice Fund. This is a fund created to acknowledge the debts owed to peoples of African descent in former British colonies and sought ways to repair the damage caused in many forms; this included funded research. This allowed me to travel across Tanzania to interview my grandmother and other indigenous elders.

Leaning on a network of East African societies, I collaborated with other doctoral students to continue the work translating and digitising scientific language into Swahili, which enabled me to publish my research in both English and Swahili, something I never thought I would do. My grandmother passed before my PhD was completed, and that broke my heart in two. I listened to the recordings of her interview on repeat as I tried to find the will to complete my research. On what would have been her 90th birthday, I completed my viva. I passed with nothing but high praise from my examiners. Fifteen years on and my grandmother's spirit is the thread that passes through all my work. To be discussing the history of my work and the future of Afro-Caribbean research alongside my peers and idols – I have her to thank for all of this. She instilled in me the curiosity, tenacity and love for the natural environment of my ancestors. So, as I step out of my hotel and onto the sand, seeing a lively group of young women aided by local children pulling a small fishing boat onto shore, I hope I've made her proud.

Afterword: For our community

De-Shaine Murray

This future and many other possibilities are attainable with you at the centre. The young person of this story could be your child, niece or nephew, cousin, friend or *you*. Keep hope and unity alive, protect and empower each other and fortify our children for the road ahead. The stories that encompass this book are acts of resistance, defiance and triumph from Black individuals who, like you, are navigating societies that have continually maligned or hindered our progress.

Despite this, we are illuminating the path towards higher educational attainment and specifically the PhD. The strength, courage and wisdom shown here is within every one of us and has allowed us to push forward irrespective of the barriers placed in our way. We ask you to dream big, aspire for greater and invest in our children's educational journeys. We have no deficit and therefore no inferiority. Racism is the principal poison that continues to curtail our advancement within the UK and globally. One antidote to this is the liberty that can be found through education. Knowledge is power and has the ability to change the lives of many.

As we fight and change the status quo from within, pushing away various obstacles, we ask you to meet us at the door. Our knowledge is powerful, our contributions matter and our scholarship is valuable in cementing our own histories, realising our individual and collective success and shaping our own futures. Let us do this hand in hand.

Index

A

academic casualisation 154
academic communities 82
  see also Black communities
academic jobs *see* employment
academic knowledge *see* lack of information
'academic limbo' (Greaves) 47
academic networks 56, 82–3, 107, 154, 155
  see also support networks
academic professional development 55
academic research 70, 154
Academic/Science Twitter 102
academic support 42, 49, 111–12, 166–7
  see also supervisors; supporting students
access to knowledge and privilege 8
Ackah, William 89
activism 168
Adi, Hakim 50
adultification 165
advice and encouragement 119–20
African-Caribbean communities 137–8
African-Caribbean Research Collective (ACRC) 47, 77–8, 135
African Diaspora Postgraduate Network (ADPN) xiii, 104–5, 106, 107
African Diaspora Religion and Culture Network 105
aggressive Black women 50, 59, 66
Ain't I a Woman (Lorde) 53
alcohol 38
alienation 107
  see also isolation
ancestral journeys 137–8

Angelou, Maya 152
annual reviews 129–30
anti-immigration state policies 50
anxiety 99, 100
Arbery, Ahmaud 78
aspirational childhoods 19–20
assertiveness and confidence 66
assisted death 127
attainment 62
attainment gap 76
attrition 168, 173
autoethnography 124
'awarding gap' 16–17

B

Bailey, Daniel 125–6
Baldwin, James 99
BAME academic staff 155
barriers 82, 123, 165–6
battle scars 169
Beckford, Robert xiii, 105–6
Beckles-Raymond, Gabriella xiii, 106
being singled out 128
belittling culture and wisdom 8–9
belonging 60–1, 169
Bioinformatics and Immunology 117
Biomedical Science 23
Birkbeck, University of London 106
Birmingham Repertory Theatre 122, 125–6
Black academic empowerment 71, 173–4
#BlackAFinSTEM 96
Black Birders Week 96, 102
Black British Academics 155
Black British and Black Caribbean women's experiences of National Health Service (NHS) 122
Black British students 10, 94

Index

Black Caribbean students 47, 77, 89, 93, 147
Black children 165
Black communities 8–9, 167–8
  collective organising 77–9
  COVID-19 pandemic 82–3
  nurturing love and validation 87–8
  refreshing and motivating 25
  resistance to oppression 72–3, 137–8
  sharing experiences 27–8, 71–2
  as supportive 88
Black Doctoral UK network 105
Black early-career researchers 154
Black feminism 53–6, 124, 146
Black immunologists 80, 83
Black in Geosciences 96, 102
Black In Immuno 80, 83–4
Black in Marine Science 96
Black in Mental Health 102
Black in Neuro 47, 78, 102–3
#BlackInSTEM 72
Black intellectual endeavour 104
Black interdisciplinary research centres of excellence 174
#BlackInTheIvory 72, 95–6, 97, 102
Black In X movements 29, 78, 83, 102
#BlackInX weeks 135
Black Lives Matter movement 7, 38, 72, 95, 101
Black majority-led departments 108
Black Muslim women 57
Blackness in research 148
Black neurodiverse scholars 164
Black PhD students 1
  as ambassadors 77
  ancestral journeys 137–8
  disrupting academic space 148
  frustrations 149
  leaving 148
  links with communities 9
  not seeing peers 78
  research priorities 174
  resilience and motivation 138
  underrepresentation 80–1, 166
  see also isolation
Black principal investigator grant holders 169
Black professors 15, 82, 159, 160
Black researchers 5, 27–8

Black people 1–9
  as commodities 5–6
  enslaved and colonised 3, 7
  exploitation and poor treatment 4
  seen as intellectually inferior 3, 81
  liminal space in British society 8
  as (non)humans 2
  in White educational space 7–8
Black Scholarship Collective 92
Black school students 4
Black scientists 81
Black Supplementary School programme 137
Black teachers 93
Black Twitter 102
Black women
  as lecturers 36
  mentors 148
  Muslim 57
  in Physics 15
  in prison 118, 119
  professors 15, 82
  in science 19
Bochner, Arthur 124
boundaries of knowledge 29
British Psychological Society 45
The broken pipeline report (Leading Routes) 77, 89, 101
Buchanan, Manzie 142
bullying 41, 63, 64, 82, 138, 172
  see also microaggressions
Butler, W.F. 150

C

career paths 35
careers services 143, 159
Casey, K. 147
Castel Verde, SS 141
'caucasities' 58
celebrating PhDs 38
Cellular and Molecular Medicine 142
centres for doctoral training (CDTs) 21, 22, 76–7
challenging inequalities and oppression 64–8
changing academic institutions 170–1
Charles, Monique 105
chartered psychologists 46
Chatham House rules 106–7
child psychologists 132
Claudia Jones Organisation 85

co-authoring papers 56
Cognitive Neuroscience 44, 131, 132
collective institutionalised racism 3
collectives 78, 167–8
Collins, P.H. 149, 154
colonialism 3, 7–8
The colour of money (Khan) 165
commiseration 161
competitive funding 143, 152–3
 see also funded opportunities
complaints 66–7, 67–8
computer science 134
conferences 56
confidence 20, 163–4
 as 'aggression'/'anger' 66
 instilled by supervisors 112, 118, 125
 isolation 49
 losing in higher education 59
 PhD interviews 33
 pride in Blackness 86
continuation rates 16
Cooper, Christian 78, 102
coping strategies 49
cost-of-living crisis 165
costs of studying 165
counternarrative storytelling 146
COVID-19 pandemic
 funding opportunities 43
 isolation 82–3
 online meetings 106
 'racial reckoning' 78
 racism 4–5
 virtual interview 43
 virtual way of life 102
Crick, Francis 81
Critical Race Theory 54, 146, 155–6, 170
Cyrus Rose 176–8

D

Dar es Salaam 177
Davis, Viola 157, 159, 161
dehumanising experiences 5
disabled students' allowances 116
disadvantaged backgrounds 165
discrimination
 deficient scrutiny 166
 degree classifications 6, 32–3
 eradicating 165
 institutional 63, 65
 and prejudice 94

disengaging from politics and societies 59
disillusionment 16, 59–60, 68, 71, 75, 116, 166
diversity 45, 50, 167
diversity admissions 99–100
DNA 81
Doctorate of Philosophy (PhD)
 see PhDs
double-consciousness 58
drama therapists 45–6
Du Bois, W.E.B. 58, 153, 159

E

early educational experiences 165
Earth Sciences 93–5, 96
East African societies 178
Economic Social Research Council 152
egalitarian opportunities 159
elite universities 6
elitism and inclusivity 87
Ellis, Carolyn 124
employment 6
 equal opportunities 159–60
 fixed-term contracts 154
 hiring practices 166
 inequalities 62
 pastoral, social equity and mentoring work 83–4
 see also work experience
empowering Black people 71, 173–4
endurance 144, 153, 169
Engineering and Physical Sciences Research Council 134
entry-level positions 159
ethnodramas 124, 126
The ethnographic I (Ellis) 124
eugenics conferences 116
Eurocentric foci 50
exclusion 86, 138
expertise 55
expressing authentic self 88
extracurricular activities 37

F

failure to complete programmes 123–4
family and friends 143–4
fear and intimidation 63, 66–7
feedback
 emerging scholars 160–1
 as intellectual violence 127–8

Index

feeling worthless 129
financial aid packages 153
financial struggles 133, 165
findaPhD.com 141, 142
first generation doctors 144
first-generation graduates 35
first-generation migrants 164
first-generation students 59, 114
fitting in 21, 49, 142, 155, 166
fixed-term contracts 154
Floyd, George 2, 7, 72, 78, 95, 101, 170
Foucault, Michel 127, 128
Franklin, Rosalind 81
funded opportunities 6, 16, 43, 77, 89, 147
see also competitive funding
funded programmes 101
funding agencies 49
see also UK Research and Innovation (UKRI)
funding applications 46–7
see also self-funding
funding Black support groups 172
see also supporting students

G

Gabriel, D. 154–5
gaslighting 61–2, 65
gatekeeping 58
Geology postgraduate researchers 93
Geophysics 94
Global Black Majorities 5, 7
grammar schools 93
grandparents 114, 141–2, 144, 176–8
grants 5
Greaves, D. 47
guidance and mentorship 167

H

Hall, S. 150
harassment 82, 138
'hidden curricula' 167
higher education 2, 6–7, 59, 107
hijabs 58
history 167
History of Africa and the African Diaspora master's course 50
holistic mentorship 172
Hong Kong 132
hooks, bell (Gloria Jean Watkins) 1, 5, 53, 86

Horizons programme (UCL) 113, 136
humanity and dignity 168–9
hypervisibility 94, 100

I

immigration threats 64
Imperial College London 3, 76–7
Imperial College London Black Doctoral Network 78
imposter syndrome 23–4, 29, 132, 141, 144, 155–6
inappropriate questions 81–2
inclusivity 38, 87
inequities 62
injustices 58
institutional biases 16
institutional discrimination 63
institutional racism 65, 68
intellectual and professional networks 56
intellectual trauma 127–8, 129
interdisciplinary subject interests 44–5
interest convergence 170
see also Critical Race Theory
international community-building 78
International Congress of Qualitative Inquiry (ICQI) 124
international students 63–4, 65–6
International Women's Day 2020. 122
internships 36–7
interviews 31, 33–4, 43, 81–2, 143
'in the meantime' guiding principle 87–8
intimidation 64
see also bullying
invisibility 100
'irruptions' (Koro-Ljungberg) 125
isolation 163–4
 ADPN helping with 107
 COVID-19 pandemic 82–3
 dwindling Black students 95
 in higher education 86, 115
 studying part-time 124
 working and studying 133
 see also Black PhD students

J

Jamaica 141–2
job advertisements 159–60
see also employment
joining collectives 135

K

Khan, O. 165
'knowledge is power' 35, 38–9, 150
knowledge production 9
Koro-Ljungberg, M. 125
Kuyateh, Oumie 102
Kwegan, Antoinette 105

L

lack of information 24–5, 85–6, 134, 143–4, 163–4
Lambeth, London 114
language barriers 164
Leading Routes 86, 87–9, 106
   The broken pipeline report 77, 89, 101
Lee, Gloria (née Meghoo) 114
Leonardo, Z. 148
Lewis, Chantelle 86, 106
liberal meritocratic universities 6
lived experiences 2–3
London 20, 26, 26–7, 105
London International Development Centre 105
Lorde, Audre 53, 63, 68
love and care 86–7

M

'mad scientist' images 20
Malta 36
managing chronic illnesses 116
marginalisation 51, 63, 64, 82, 154
masks of performance 58–60
maternity leave 120
medical schools 30
Medical Science 23
mediocrity 98
mental health 41, 42, 98–9, 171–2
mentors 37–8
merit
   being chosen on 121
   succeeding on 6
microaffirmation 155
microaggressions 16, 41, 42, 61, 94, 95
   see also bullying
milestones and checkpoints 173
minorities 38, 104, 111
Minorities in STEM 27–8
minority taxes 168
misdiagnoses 4
mistreated in society 2

moments of dissociating clarity 53–4
Morris, Bernard and Maureen 142
Morris, Gloria 142
Morris, Joseph 141, 144
motivations 30, 138
multi-layered discrimination 50–1
multiple identities 164
Muslim 38, 50–1, 57, 59
   student 38
   woman/women 50, 57, 59, 61

N

navigating higher education 59
'navigational capital' (Yasso) 148
networks *see* academic networks; support networks
Neuroaesthetics 45, 46
neurodiversity 164
neuroscience 134
NHS 123
Nine Mile, St Ann, Jamaica 113
non-White researchers 27
novel research 49
nurturing environments 105

O

Office for Students 107
online focus groups 10
Open University 118, 119
oppressive working environments 63
oral traditions 146
organising events 56
othering, anti-Blackness, anti-Muslimness, gatekeeping 58
outcomes 62
outreach programmes 77, 114–15, 117, 133, 164
overworking 99
Oxbridge 20–1

P

panic attacks 128–9
parental support 100
part-time jobs 133
passive Muslim women stereotypes 50
pastoral support 55
   see also supervisors
patriarchal Whiteness 147
performative autoethnography 122
performative diversity 16
personal support systems 116
pharmaceutical companies 31–2, 33

Index

PhDs 1
  accessing 163–4
  barriers to 82, 123, 165–6
  being excited and curious 29
  demystifying 173
  downgrading to MPhil 129–30
  exclusive to the elite 21
  project adverts 142–4
  selection processes 166
  surviving 59, 60, 149–50
  as swimming 146–50
  understanding 134, 143–4
  waiting for opportunities 27, 28
PhD applications
  advice 55, 119–20
  cycle 16
  interviews 34
  naïve approaches 116–17
  networks 21–2, 91
  rejections 16, 23, 32, 37–8, 90
  and supervisors 42–3
  transparency and uniformity 171
  writing 142–3
PhD Hive 135
PhD journeys 40, 109, 144–5, 158, 162
PhD studentships
  remuneration 165
  research groups' dominant culture 166
  UKRI awards 77, 89, 146
physical, mental, emotional and relational challenges 144
physical sciences 76
Physics 20
pity 161
placements 37, 42, 142
  see also work experience
poetry 57
postgraduate researcher representative (PGR rep) 64–5
pregnancies 120
presentations 33–4
primary schools 20
principal investigators 166
principles and values 62
prisons 4, 120
'problematic natives' 3
professional networks 56
promising changes 76
Psychology 45
Psychology of the Arts, Neuroaesthetics and Creativity 46
publishing 154

R

race and gender 94
racial microaggressions 2, 16
racism 2–3, 4
  in academia 61, 99, 165
  Black people seen as intellectually inferior 3, 81
  and gaslighting 61–2
  halting progression 169
  personalising 61
  schools 40–1
  and sexism 164
  tackling 87, 172
  'ticking all the boxes' 94, 96
  University of Leeds 94
reading groups 56
reading lists 55, 56
reassurance 121
recognition 169
redefining success 87
rejected applications 16, 23, 32, 37–8, 90
  see also PhD applications
Reparatory Justice Fund 177–8
research assistants 42
research collectives 56
research development opportunities 153–4
research groups 166
research scientists 23
resilience 138
resisting marginalisation 51
resisting oppression 137
rheumatoid arthritis 116
Rivas, Althea-Maria 107
Rodney, W. 10
Rollock, N. 15
Runnymede Trust 165
Russell Group 85–6

S

Samuels, Pansy 142
scholarships 165
School of Oriental and African Studies 3
schools 16, 20, 40–1, 44–5, 115
Science, Technology, Engineering, and Mathematics (STEM) 27
secondary schools 20, 44–5
second-guessing 104
self-confidence 119
self-editing 58

self-funding 152–3
  see also funding applications
sensorimotor and dance research 46
setting expectations 117
sexism 164
  see also racism
silenced Muslim women 59
Smith, L.T. 148
social media 82, 83, 102
social science researchers and lecturers 158
societal prejudices 16
socio-economic divisions 115
Somalis 90, 91–2
specialised support 159
spirit of community 88
staying and belonging 60–1
stereotypes 165
Stoke Newington, London 85
storytelling 57, 146
structural issues 75
struggling for recognition 155
student ambassadors 116
Student Finance England (SFE) 116, 117
studentships 165
supervisors 136
  being reported to 64
  being supportive 55, 120–1, 122–6, 132–5
  choosing 53–4, 134
  educating and training 172
  feedback 55, 124
  focus on Blackness 55–6
  hostile criticisms 129–30
  hostile relationships 128
  humanity and dignity 168–9
  panic attacks 128–9
  pastoral support 55
  relationships with 90–1, 144
  see also academic support
supporting students 34, 43, 136
  academic institutions 49
  for Black scientists 83
  family and friends 143–4
  and mental health 171–2
  teaching assistants 36
  unsatisfactory results 76
  see also academic support
support networks 10, 28–9, 56, 82–3, 90–2
  see also academic networks

support systems 65, 111, 113, 116, 117, 138
surviving PhDs 59, 60, 149–50
symposia 56

T

Tanzania 176–7
Tate, S. 154–5
Taylor, Breonna 78, 95, 101
technology 132–3
textbooks 29
Theatre and Psychology 45
third-generation university students 42
threats 58
'ticking all the boxes' comments 94, 96
toxic culture 75, 82, 107, 136, 167
transparency 117
tribes *see* Black communities
trivialisation 155
Tubman, Harriet 157, 159
Turkey 36–7
Twitter 83, 96, 102

U

UK Research and Innovation (UKRI) 77, 89, 107, 147
  see also funding agencies
unbelonging 61
uncertainties 163–4
unconventional strategies 148
undergraduate students 42, 76, 80
underrepresentation 80–1, 166
understanding PhDs 134, 143–4
  see also lack of information
unemployment 160
  see also employment
unequal power dynamics 81
universities
  careers services 143, 159
  collective institutionalised racism 3
  collegiate system 24
  discriminatory practices 6–7
  functions 87
  rich academic environments 158
University College London Horizons programme 113, 136
University of Birmingham 76
University of Bristol 142
University of Chichester 50
University of Leeds 94, 96
University of Liverpool 94–5

Index

university politics and societies 59
unlawful discrimination 65
Unlearning Racism in Geoscience (URGE) 96
unpaid internships 37
unspoken rules 167
USA 54

V

victimisation 64
virtual interviews 43
virtual reality 102, 132–3
visibility 2
vivas 107, 125, 144, 178

W

Watkins, Gloria Jean (bell hooks) 1, 5, 53, 86
Watson, James 81–2
Webb, Lincoln & Jennifer 114
Webb, Viola (née Lawrence) 113–14
'weighted recognition' 15–16
'weighted waiting' 16, 48

West African Research Collective (WARC) 28, 77–8, 101–2
White academics 101, 138
White knowledge systems 150
White-majority schools 142
Whiteness 147–9
White supremacists 116
White university space 115
widening participation initiatives 16
Williams, P. 147
Williams, Paulette 106
Windrush generation 113–14, 141–2
wisdom and knowledge 85
work experience 24, 27, 31–2, 33, 37–8, 133
  see also employment; placements
worthiness 121
wraparound structures 165
writing applications 142–3
  see also PhD applications

Y

Yosso, T.J. 148
young Black Muslim women 50–1

www.ingramcontent.com/pod-product-compliance
Lightning Source LLC
Chambersburg PA
CBHW051546020426
42333CB00016B/2115